Vernon Coleman's Commonplace Book

Vernon Coleman

Books by Vernon Coleman include:

Medical
The Medicine Men
Paper Doctors
Everything You Want To Know About Ageing
The Home Pharmacy
Aspirin or Ambulance
Face Values
Stress and Your Stomach
A Guide to Child Health
Guilt
The Good Medicine Guide
An A to Z of Women's Problems
Bodypower
Bodysense
Taking Care of Your Skin
Life without Tranquillisers
High Blood Pressure
Diabetes
Arthritis
Eczema and Dermatitis
The Story of Medicine
Natural Pain Control
Mindpower
Addicts and Addictions
Dr Vernon Coleman's Guide to Alternative Medicine
Stress Management Techniques
Overcoming Stress
The Health Scandal
The 20 Minute Health Check
Sex for Everyone
Mind over Body
Eat Green Lose Weight
Why Doctors Do More Harm Than Good
The Drugs Myth
Complete Guide to Sex

How to Conquer Backache
How to Conquer Pain
Betrayal of Trust
Know Your Drugs
Food for Thought
The Traditional Home Doctor
Relief from IBS
The Parent's Handbook
Men in Bras, Panties and Dresses
Power over Cancer
How to Conquer Arthritis
How to Stop Your Doctor Killing You
Superbody
Stomach Problems – Relief at Last
How to Overcome Guilt
How to Live Longer
Coleman's Laws
Millions of Alzheimer Patients Have Been Misdiagnosed
Climbing Trees at 112
Is Your Health Written in the Stars?
The Kick-Ass A–Z for over 60s
Briefs Encounter
The Benzos Story
Dementia Myth

Psychology/Sociology
Stress Control
How to Overcome Toxic Stress
Know Yourself (1988)
Stress and Relaxation
People Watching
Spiritpower
Toxic Stress
I Hope Your Penis Shrivels Up
Oral Sex: Bad Taste and Hard To Swallow
Other People's Problems
The 100 Sexiest, Craziest, Most Outrageous Agony Column Questions (and Answers) Of All Time

How to Relax and Overcome Stress
Too Sexy To Print
Psychiatry
Are You Living With a Psychopath?

Politics and General
England Our England
Rogue Nation
Confronting the Global Bully
Saving England
Why Everything Is Going To Get Worse Before It Gets Better
The Truth They Won't Tell You...About The EU
Living In a Fascist Country
How to Protect & Preserve Your Freedom, Identity & Privacy
Oil Apocalypse
Gordon is a Moron
The OFPIS File
What Happens Next?
Bloodless Revolution
2020
Stuffed
The Shocking History of the EU
Coming Apocalypse
Covid-19: The Greatest Hoax in History
Old Man in a Chair
Endgame
Proof that Masks do more harm than Good
Covid-19: The Fraud Continues
Covid-19: Exposing the Lies
Social Credit: Nightmare on Your Street
NHS: What's wrong and how to put it right
They want your money and your life.
Their Terrifying Plan

Diaries and Autobiographies
Diary of a Disgruntled Man
Just another Bloody Year
Bugger off and Leave Me Alone

Return of the Disgruntled Man
Life on the Edge
The Game's Afoot
Tickety Tonk
Memories 1
Memories 2
Memories 3
My Favourite Books
Truth Teller: The Price

Animals
Why Animal Experiments Must Stop
Fighting For Animals
Alice and Other Friends
Animal Rights – Human Wrongs
Animal Experiments – Simple Truths

General Non Fiction
How to Publish Your Own Book
How to Make Money While Watching TV
Strange but True
Daily Inspirations
Why Is Public Hair Curly
People Push Bottles Up Peaceniks
Secrets of Paris
Moneypower
101 Things I Have Learned
100 Greatest Englishmen and Englishwomen
Cheese Rolling, Shin Kicking and Ugly Tattoos
One Thing after Another
Vernon Coleman's Dictionary of Old English Words and Phrases
Old Man in an Old Car

Novels (General)
Mrs Caldicot's Cabbage War
Mrs Caldicot's Knickerbocker Glory
Mrs Caldicot's Oyster Parade
Mrs Caldicot's Turkish Delight

Deadline
Second Chance
Tunnel
Mr Henry Mulligan
The Truth Kills
Revolt
My Secret Years with Elvis
Balancing the Books
Doctor in Paris
Stories with a Twist in the Tale (short stories)
Dr Bullock's Annals
The Awakening of Dr Amelia Leighton
A Needle for a Needle (novella)

The Young Country Doctor Series
Bilbury Chronicles
Bilbury Grange
Bilbury Revels
Bilbury Country
Bilbury Village
Bilbury Pie (short stories)
Bilbury Pudding (short stories)
Bilbury Tonic
Bilbury Relish
Bilbury Mixture
Bilbury Delights
Bilbury Joys
Bilbury Tales
Bilbury Days
Bilbury Memories

Novels (Sport)
Thomas Winsden's Cricketing Almanack
Diary of a Cricket Lover
The Village Cricket Tour
The Man Who Inherited a Golf Course
Around the Wicket
Too Many Clubs and Not Enough Balls

Cat books
Alice's Diary
Alice's Adventures
We Love Cats
Cats Own Annual
The Secret Lives of Cats
Cat Basket
The Cataholics' Handbook
Cat Fables
Cat Tales
Catoons from Catland

As Edward Vernon
Practice Makes Perfect
Practise What You Preach
Getting Into Practice
Aphrodisiacs – An Owner's Manual
The Complete Guide to Life

Play
Mrs Caldicot's Cabbage War

Written with Donna Antoinette Coleman
How to Conquer Health Problems between Ages 50 & 120
Health Secrets Doctors Share With Their Families
Animal Miscellany
England's Glory
Wisdom of Animals

Copyright Vernon Coleman September 2024
The right of Vernon Coleman to be identified as the author of this work has been asserted in accordance with the Copyright, Designs and Patents Act 1988.

To Antoinette

You are so kind, so gentle and so sensitive that you tremble in the storms of life – always worrying more about other people than yourself. But you are so brave that you refuse to bow your head. You are all the world I want. And all the world I could ever need. All my beautiful memories from the past are with you. All my beautiful memories from the future will be with you. All my happiness comes from my love for you. It is my privilege to give you my love for eternity. Nothing else matters a damn. You are constantly in my heart, always on my mind.

Thank you for being you
And for everything you do
With all my love
Always and All Ways

Preface

In olden times (before even I was born) it was customary for ladies and gentlemen to keep a scrap book containing items they'd collected from books, magazines and newspapers. They'd add in quotes and snippets from conversation they had remembered and wanted to write down to keep. Those volumes were called 'commonplace' books.

My commonplace book contains stories, anecdotes, lists, comments, quotes, etc., which I think you'll enjoy. (The quotes are not the sort which can be dug out of a Book of Quotations! I have only consulted my books of quotations to check on quotes I remembered or had jotted down. The un-credited quotes are entirely my own responsibility.) The book also includes some of my recollections and idle thoughts. I hope you'll find new facts, thought-provoking opinions and titbits of information which will make you want to say: 'Hey, listen to this…!'

Vernon Coleman
Bilbury, September 2024

John McNab

John Buchan wrote some of the world's first (and best thrillers) with *The Thirty Nine Steps* being the best known. But for many aficionados his greatest book is one called *John McNab*, a novel which tells the story of three eminent and highly successful friends in their 40s who confess to one another that they are bored with their lives. One is a lawyer and Member of Parliament, a second is a banker and third is a Cabinet Minister. Their doctor advises them to do something exciting and dangerous in order to put a little spice into their humdrum lives. They decide to try poaching in Scotland. Sharing the name John McNab, they set up base in Scotland and write to three landowners advising them that they intend to kill a stag or a salmon on the landowner's land between two specific dates. If they fail they will pay a forfeit and if they succeed they will give £50 to charity. Two landowners accept the challenge and the third sends a legal letter threatening to sue. The three friends have many adventures and regain their zest for life. That's the novel. But Buchan's story wasn't entirely fiction. In 1897, a young army officer called Captain James Brander Dunbar was miffed that he had not received an invitation to go stalking that summer, and remarked that if things didn't improve he would try poaching. He boasted that he could kill a stag in any forest in Scotland. (Dunbar was what might be called a bit of a lad. By the time he died at the age of 95 in 1969, he had fathered 19 illegitimate children and was described by a relative as 'not being a good husband', which is probably something of an understatement.) The boast was met by the 4th Baron Abinger who bet Dunbar £20 that he couldn't take a stag off his 42,000 acre estate. Despite the best efforts of the Baron's men, Dunbar succeeded in killing a stag and delivering the head to the Baron's house. He was duly rewarded with a cheque for £20. These days, the John McNab story has become reality and the modern McNab involves killing a stag, a salmon, and a brace of grouse within 24 hours – though not necessarily illegally and without the landowner's permission. There is a junior McNab which consists of catching a trout, a rabbit and a pigeon and a politically incorrect Royal McNab which consists of adding the laird's cook or housekeeper to the classic trio. The North highland McNab consists of a stag, a goose and a brown trout. For those who can't travel outside London there is a special McNab consisting of a pike, a pigeon and a rabbit and there is a rather pitiful vegetarian McNab consisting of three types of field mushroom.

Pen names

Many (if not most) professional authors use pen names – usually when they want to write books in a style or genre which is notably different to the style or genre for which they are known. Several well-known writers write successful series of books under different names. So, for example, Donald E.Westlake also wrote under the name Richard Stark and numerous books under both names were filmed (he used at least eight other names but those were the two most successful) and Evan Hunter was also Ed McBain (though neither of those nom de plumes was the name he was born with). Actors and actresses are usually stuck with the name with which they start out with but writers have much more freedom. One of the most successful authors to use multiple pen names was Roger Longrigg who wrote 55 books and who used different pseudonyms for each style and persona. He used the name Laura Black for romantic historical novels (she was made an honorary daughter of Mark Twain by the American Mark Twain Society) and he became Ivor Drummond when he wrote thrillers set in the world of luxury yachts and race meetings. When he was Domini Taylor he wrote cold-blooded black comedies about dysfunctional families. As Frank Parrish he was awarded the John Cheever mystery writer's prize for a first novel (though in fact it was Longrigg's 20th book). There were a number of other names in his repertoire but his most extraordinary persona was 'Rosalind Erskine' who was supposed to be a 17-year-old schoolgirl. Her first book appeared in 1962 (when Longrigg was actually 33-years-old) and it was a raunchy novel about a group of boarding school girls who turned their school gym into a brothel. The photograph of Miss Erskine which appeared on the cover was shot from the side with the head turned away and looks as though it could have been a photograph of Longrigg wearing a rather ropey wig, though I offer my apologies if the model was actually a 17-year-old girl with lovely hair who had been hired for the purpose. Miss Erskine's hobbies were listed as practising with her 9 mm Luger automatic. Sadly, the truth was revealed when a journalist guessed that Longrigg was the real author (the giveaway was apparently that Longrigg's middle name was Erskine). However, most of Longrigg's many pseudonyms remained secrets and all were successful, with quite a number of his books adapted for the stage or television. Just how he kept track of who he was and what was happening to his various pen names is the one remaining mystery. A nice touch is that when Longrigg's stable of authors received mail from his readers, he replied in character. Saucy letters written to Miss Erskine received a suitably saucy reply.

Lady Winchelsea – Too Poorly to see the Doctor

In 1903, the family of a Lady Winchelsea called a doctor to see her. But when the doctor arrived, Lady Winchelsea sent down a message to say that she was too ill to see him. (This curious story reminds me that when I was a GP I had a very frail and elderly partner who found stairs too difficult to manage. When visiting patients who were in bed upstairs, he would stand at the bottom of the stairs and shout up his questions. He would send a relative or neighbour up the stairs to take a temperature or a pulse.)

The Cure

'It is from nature that the disease arises and from nature comes the cure, not from the physician.' – *Paracelsus*

Technology

'We tend to overestimate the effect of technology in the short term and underestimate the effect in the long term.' – *Roy Amara*

Profanity

'Under certain circumstances profanity provides a relief denied even to prayer.' – *Mark Twain*

Younghusband

When Francis Younghusband, (philosopher, soldier, adventurer and spy) was posted to Tibet in 1903, his luggage filled 29 cases including a container exclusively for hats. As an English gentleman, he naturally had proper dress for every occasion. His clothes at Tuna included, among other things, eighteen pairs of boots and shoes, twenty-eight pairs of socks, thirty-two collars, and sixty-seven shirts, some flannel, others white, twilled or coloured, along with studs and any number of ties. He had a dozen suits with matching waistcoats. His twelve winter overcoats included a Chinese fur, a chesterfield, an ulster, a posteen (a type of pelisse or long coat made with leather with the fleece attached), two Jaegers and a waterproof coat. His hats included a white helmet and khaki and brown felt hats, two forage caps, a white Panama, a cocked hat, both a thick and thin solar topi and, finally, a shikar, intended only to be used when shooting partridges in the Chumbi Valley.

A Short List of All Round Sportsmen and Women

These days sportsmen and sportswomen tend to specialise. Someone who plays international football won't usually expect to be selected for their national cricket team and won't expect to win one of the tennis grand-slam tournaments. Indeed, specialisation is so extreme that players in team sports will be expected to stick to a specific position within the team. So a footballer might play at full back (or whatever they call it this week) and nowhere else, and a cricketer may be included in a team solely for his leg break bowling.

Things weren't always like this.

Dr Kevin O'Flanagan played Gaelic football at school and then turned to soccer and became an international at seventeen. He played soccer for Arsenal and Ireland. He also played international rugby for Ireland and won national championships as a sprinter and long jumper.

R.L.Baker was one of Australia's leading Rugby players, runners, swimmers, rowers and horsemen – winning prizes and awards in all those sports.

Lottie Dod won the Wimbledon singles tennis title in 1887 at the age of 15. She won the title five times before retiring and turning to golf. She then won the national golf championship. She also played international hockey and was a top skater and archer.

Major J.W.H.T.Douglas is still remembered as one of England's most successful all round cricketers. He captained England at cricket and played football for the England amateur side. At school he took up boxing and won the middleweight gold medal at the 1908 Olympic Games.

Maxwell Woosnam captained England at lawn tennis in the Davis club and won the Wimbledon doubles title with Randolph Lycett in 1921. He also captained England at association football and was the captain of Manchester City football club. He played real tennis for England and played cricket for Cambridge.

Babe Didrickson was a successful international tennis player, athlete, golfer and billiard player. She also played basketball and baseball at top level. In 1932 she qualified for five Olympic events but was only allowed to compete in three. She achieved world records in all of them. In 1946-7 she won 17 golf tournaments in a row including the American and British championships. She was selected for an All American basketball team.

C.B.Fry captained England at cricket and played football for England too. He held the world's record for the long jump and in his seventies was still able to leap backwards, from a stationary position, on to a mantelpiece. Fry was also an excellent golfer, shot putter, ice skater, hammer thrower and rugby player. (He played rugby for Oxford University.) Fry was a writer, teacher, publisher and renowned broadcaster (appearing regularly on a programme called The Brains Trust.) He was offered the throne of Albania (but turned it down) and to relax would read books in Greek and Latin. He had the rank of captain in the Royal Naval Reserve and was Captain Superintendent of a Royal Navy training ship. Fry stood as a Liberal candidate for Parliament in 1922 and narrowly lost.

More recently, it used to be not uncommon for sports stars to play both cricket and football. So, for example, Denis Compton one of England's most successful cricketers, also played football for England and Arsenal. M.J.K.Smith played both rugby and cricket for England. As recently as the 1950s, sports stars were not well paid and Arthur Milton, who was the last sportsman to play both cricket and football for England, became a postman after his retirement and later delivered free newspapers in the Bristol area.

Freedom
'Money is minted freedom.' – *Fyodor Dostoevsky*

Aussie Speaks Up
In 2010 I was sent a copy of a letter which an anonymous Australian had sent to the Australian Government. Here it is:

Dear Mr Minister

I am in the process of renewing my passport, and still cannot believe this.

How is it that K-Mart has my address and telephone number, and knows that I bought a television set and set of golf clubs from them back in 1997 and yet the Federal Government is still asking me where I was born and on what date?

Do you guys do this by hand?

My birth date you have in my Medicare information and it is on all the income tax forms I've filed for the last 40 years. It is on my driver's licence, on the last eight passports I've ever had, on all those stupid customs declarations forms I've had to fill out before being allowed off the planes over the last 30 years, and all those insufferable census forms that I've filled out every five years since 1966.

Also, would somebody please take note, once and for all, that my mother's name is Audrey, my father's name is Jack and I'd be absolutely fucking astounded if that ever changed between now and when I drop dead.

I apologise Mr Minister. But I'm really pissed off this morning. Between you and me I've had enough of all this bullshit. You send the application to my house, then you ask me for my fucking address! What the hell is going on with your mob? Have you got a gang of mindless Neanderthal arseholes working there?

And another thing, look at my damned picture. Do I look like Bin Laden? I can't even grow a beard for God's sake. I just want to go to New Zealand and see my new granddaughter. And would someone please tell me, why would you give a shit whether I plan on visiting a farm in the next 15 days. If I ever got the urge to do something weird to a sheep or a horse, believe me I'd sure as hell not want to tell anyone.

Well, I have to go now, because I have to go to the other end of the city and get another fucking copy of my birth certificate and part with another $80 for the privilege of accessing my own information. Would it be so complicated to have all the services in the same spot, to assist in the issuance of a new passport on the same day?

Nooooo…that'd be too fucking easy and makes far too much sense. You would much prefer to have us running all over the place like chickens with our fucking heads cut off and then having to find some high society wanker to confirm that it's really me in the damned photo. You know the photo, the one where we're not allowed to smile.

Signed

An Irate Australian Citizen

P.S. Remember what I said about the picture, and getting someone in high society to confirm that it's me? Well, my family has been in this country before 1850 and I have served in the regular Army for over 30 years and still have high security clearances. However, your rules require that I have to get someone 'important' to verify who I am – someone like my doctor, who was born and raised in Pakistan. You are all idiots.

Luck
In most people's lives the good luck and the bad luck cancel one another out – and the trick is to try to take the greatest possible advantage of all the good luck so that you can ride all the bad luck.

BBC
Paying the BBC licence fee is an act of treachery. Working for the BBC is an act of treason.

Discredited
Since Google decided to describe me as a discredited conspiracy theorist (with no evidence whatsoever for the libel) scores of publishers and hundreds of booksellers in 26 countries have banned my books. Since I have earned my living as an author for many decades, the only solution has been to publish my own books. Even so, many of my self-published books have been banned by online outlets. Telling the truth has destroyed my career, my reputation, my income, my health and much else besides. But I wouldn't change a thing.

Calories
While checking on the calorie contents of various foods I was puzzled by the discovery that whereas one slice of white bread contains 235 calories, a slice of toasted white bread contains 265 calories. Why and how, I wonder, does the process of toasting add energy value to a piece of bread? I checked with another book of calories and it too maintained that toast contains more calories than the bread from which it was made.

Photos
The average smart phone owner now takes between 5,000 and 15,000 photographs a year – many of them selfies. It is now possible to hire a specialist to sort through your photographs, pick out the ones worth keeping and categorise them. The average number of videos taken is considerably smaller but still disconcertingly high. What do people do with all these photographs? Why do they need to take so many? Someone who starts taking photos at the age of 20 and stops at the age of 70 will have probably taken half a million pictures of themselves hugging strangers and admiring their food.

Seven Doctors who wrote books
Robert Bridges
Arthur Conan Doyle
Oliver Goldsmith
John Keats
Somerset Maugham
Francois Rabelais
Tobias Smollett

Ambrose Bierce's Last Days.
'If you hear of my being stood up against a Mexican stone wall and shot to rags please know that I think that is a pretty good way to depart this life. It beats old age, disease, or falling down the cellar stairs. To be a gringo in Mexico – ah, that is euthanasia.' – *(Ambrose Bierce, author of the Devil's Dictionary and brilliant short stories, travelled to Mexico when he was in his seventies. He was present at the Battle of Tierra Blanca with Pancho Villa and disappeared in 1913. No one knows exactly what happened to him.)*

Sepsis

These days, hospitals usually advise post-operative patients to be on the look-out for signs of septicaemia. This is wise but the thing about septicaemia is that it develops very quickly. It can kill a healthy individual in hours. But it can be cured if you're fast. And the treatment of choice is very simple: a broad spectrum antibiotic. The official NHS advice is that treatment for sepsis needs to be started within an hour.

Sepsis is a major problem today. Worldwide, it is now said that one in five deaths around the world is caused by sepsis (an infection in the blood). More people die of sepsis than die of cancer. It is a huge and widely ignored problem.

Now that most GPs work part time (in Britain the average GP works 23-24 hours a week) and most small hospitals have been closed, the majority of individuals live over an hour away from the nearest hospital – even if they have access to a driver and a fast car – and so this presents a real problem. Ambulance services are patchy, to say the least, and in Britain, even in emergencies, ambulances can take many hours (even days) to arrive. And once patients arrive at their nearest Accident and Emergency Department, they may have to wait many hours or days to be seen. (That is no exaggeration.)

After Antoinette had an operation I asked our GP if she would give us a prescription for some antibiotic tablets – only to be taken if sepsis developed. The symptoms and signs aren't hard to spot.

Our GP refused. 'It's not something we would do,' she said, rather pompously. 'We're always here for you', she added, which was, of course, a lie because, as I've noted before, the surgery is open more or less the same hours as the local public library is and it would be a considerable exaggeration to say that the library is always there for us.

Hospitals or GPs should give patients a starter dose of antibiotics for emergencies. If they are worried about antibiotics being abused they should put the starter dose in a sealed pack that had to be returned if unused. I have been fighting against the overprescribing of antibiotics since the 1970s but this is a serious problem.

Genes

'Of course we can splice genes. But can we not splice genes?' – *Jean Paul Sartre*

A Personal Philosophy

'I have a simple philosophy. Fill what's empty, empty what's full, and scratch what itches.' – *Alice Roosevelt Longworth*

GPs

When I was a GP we used to visit patients who went home after surgery. Sometimes, we visited them while they were in hospital too since even there we were responsible for their health. Frail, elderly patients living at home were visited every two weeks. It all seemed part of the job and the right thing to do. These days most GPs never ever visit their patients at home. It is no wonder that the relationship between doctors and patients has completely broken down. .

The Waverley Novels

Sir Walter Scott's first novel was called Waverley. His subsequent novels were attributed to 'The Author of Waverley' and are therefore known as the Waverley Novels. Scott's novels were nearly all written anonymously though his identity became known after a decade or so.

Mount Everest

Everest has been growing at a rate of a centimetre a year for the last few centuries. This means that the people who climb it this year will have to climb further than the mountaineers who climbed it a decade ago.

Portmeirion
Portmeirion is an Italianate village on the coast of North Wales. It was designed and built by Sir Clouch Williams-Ellis between 1925 and 1976 and is famous as the site of *The Prisoner* series on television; a legendary series starring Patrick McGoohan as prisoner Number Six. Williams-Ellis was rather eccentric and, twenty years after his death, in accordance with his will, some of his ashes were placed inside a firework and sent into the night sky over the Portmeirion estuary.

French newspapers
French newspapers used to have a part of one or more pages given over to light literature or criticism. These were called feuilletons. It is, I hope, no exaggeration to describe this book as a collection of miniature feuilletons.

Stamps
England invented postage stamps and so England's stamps are the only ones which carry no national identification other than the monarch's picture or silhouette. Time and longitude are both measured from Greenwich in England.

Best Movie Thrillers
Thirty Nine Steps
Third Man
Casablanca

Intangibles

'We make walls, floor, roof, doors and windows for a room. But it is the empty space within that makes the room liveable. Thus, while the tangible have advantages it is the intangible that makes it useful.' – *Lao Tzu*

Valets

'I only took with me two valets and a cook.' – *The Marechal de Biron, reporting his imprisonment in the Bastille in 1631*

Tattoos

'I attribute my whole success in life to a rigid observance of a fundamental rule; never have yourself tattooed with any woman's name, not even her initials.' – *P.G.Wodehouse*

Wilkie Collins author of 'Rambles Beyond Railways' (1851)

I wrote a book detailing my favourite 100 non-fiction books. If I ever write a second book detailing another 100 favourite non-fiction books, the first volume on the new list will be *Rambles Beyond Railways* by Wilkie Collins. Mr Collins was an English novelist, short story writer, playwright and writer of non-fiction. He is best remembered for *The Moonstone* and *The Woman in White* and was one of the most successful authors of the 19th century. In 1851, Collins, together with a peripatetic companion, an artist, travelled to the then fairly unknown county of Cornwall and wrote a revealing book about his peregrinations. He watched locals harvesting pilchards, went down a tin mine and explored many local legends. When the second edition of the book appeared, Collins wrote an apology which read: 'Since this work first appeared, the all-conquering Railway has invaded Cornwall; and the title of my book has become a misnomer already. Am I willing to change it? Certainly not. It was strictly descriptive of the state of the county, when my companion and I walked through Cornwall – it marks the period and is connected with the remembrance of our tour – and it has an attaching influence for me as being associated with a book which has been very kindly received by the public. For these reasons, I am obstinately bent on letting my title remain. The Cornish Railway Company may be a very powerful company, and may extend their present line from Penzance, till they reach Plymouth – they may make St Michael's Mount a site for a monster engine house; and may establish a Board of Directors on top of the Logan Rock – but there is one thing they shan't do: they shan't make me change my Title. A certain Abbe wrote a book, in the time of Gustavus III to prove that nothing could overthrow the Swedish Constitution of that period. Just as he was correcting his last proof sheet, a gentleman rushed into the room, and said that the Constitution had been utterly annulled. 'Sir,' replied the Abbe, looking up very quietly, 'they may overthrow the Constitution, but they can't overthrow MY BOOK,' and he went on with his work. With this case in point, and the authority of an Abbe to back me, I say once again – they may make a Railway in Cornwall; but they can't make an alteration to MY TITLE.

How the people of Looe got rid of their rats – Wilkie Collins

A plague of rats invaded the Cornish town of Looe in the 19th century. In his book, Wilkie Collins explained how the locals had dealt with their problem. Ordinary methods had failed. It was said that rats left for dead had mysteriously revived and that wounded rats had gone to ground, convalesced and returned to annoy the locals. 'The great problem,' wrote Collins, 'was not how to kill the rats but how to annihilate them so effectually that the whole population might certainly know that the re-appearance even of one of them was altogether out of the question. This was the problem and it was solved in the following manner: All of the available inhabitants of the town were called to join in a great hunt. The rats were caught by every conceivable artifice; and, once taken, were instantly and ferociously smothered in onions; the corpses were then decently laid out on clean china dishes, and straightway eaten with vindictive relish by the people of Looe. Never was any invention for destroying rats so complete and so successful as this! Every man, woman and child who could eat, could swear to the death and annihilation of all the rats they had eaten. Day after Day, passed on, and rats disappeared by hundreds never to return. What could all their cunning and resolution avail them now? They had resisted before, and could have resisted still, the ordinary force of dogs, ferrets, traps, sticks, stones and guns, arrayed against them; but when to these engines of assault were added smothering onions, scalding stew-pans, hungry mouths, sharp teeth, good digestions, and the gastric juice, what could they do but give in? Swift and sure was the destruction that now overwhelmed them – everybody who wanted a dinner had a strong personal interest in hunting them down to the very last. In a short space of time the island was cleared of the usurpers. Cheeses remained entire; ricks rose uninjured. And this is the true story of how the people of Looe got rid of the rats.'

Pilchard Fishing

Wilkie Collins also wrote about Cornish pilchard fishing. In the 19th century, fishing for pilchards was a major source of income for the Cornish. A man would stand on the cliff and look out for shoals of pilchards. When he announced that he could see a suitable shoal, in suitable waters, the fishermen would go out and circle the fish with a massive net. Afterwards the local women would salt the fish to preserve them. And then the pilchards would be put into barrels to be sold. The importance of the pilchard industry to the Cornish people cannot be over emphasised. Collins investigated the pilchard fishing in some detail, talked to those involved and described how 'the rich tribute of the great deep is most generously lavished on the land which most needs a compensation for its own sterility'. Here is a taste of what Collins had to say about the Cornish pilchard fishing industry: 'Some idea of the almost incalculable multitude of pilchards caught on the shores of Cornwall, may be formed from the following data. At the small fishing cove of Trereen, 600 hogsheads were taken in little more than one week, during August 1850. Allowing 2,400 fish only to each hogshead (3,000 would be the highest calculation) we have a result of 1,440,000 pilchards caught by the inhabitants of one little village alone, on the Cornish coast, at the commencement of the season's fishing! At considerable sea port towns, where there is an unusually large supply of men, boats and nets, such figures as those quoted above are far below the mark. At St Ives, for example, 1,000 hogsheads were taken in the first three nets cast into the water. The number of hogsheads exported annually, averages 22,000. In 1850, 27,000 were secured for the foreign markets.'

Sardines
For marketing purposes, pilchards were subsequently re-named sardines.

Dreams
Dreams and memories are there to protect you from the dull and savage days.

Guests
'Guests are like fish – they go off after three days.' – *Alan Plater*

Work
'It's probably true that hard work never killed anyone, but I figure why take the chance?' – *Ronald Reagan*

Truth
'Tell the truth and you are likely to be a pariah within your family, a semi-criminal to authorities and damned with faint praise by your peers. So why do we do it? Because saying what you think is the only freedom.' – *Erica Jong*

The Scoop
American ships used to throw information capsules overboard as they passed near to the Skellig Islands off Ireland. Boys in small boats would fish out the capsules and deliver them to journalists. And thus the phrase 'get the scoop' was invented. It was through this system that England first learned of the assassination of Abraham Lincoln in 1865.

Six politically incorrect authors
Mickey Spillane
Frank Richards
John Buchan
Sapper
Dornford Yates
Ian Fleming
All these authors wrote brilliant books which are now disapproved of by the woke and therefore doubly worth reading and highly recommended. Look for the shudder of disapproval if you ask your local bookseller or librarian to find a book by one of these authors.

Georges Simenon
Georges Simenon is recognised as one of the greatest authors of the 20th century. Here is an edited extract from an interview with Carvel Collins which appeared in *The Paris Review* and which explains how

Simenon worked.

'As soon as I have the beginnings I can't bear it very long; so the next day I take my envelope (Simenon made initial notes for each book on a manila envelope), take my telephone book for names, and take my town map – you know, to see exactly where things happen. And two days later I begin writing. And the beginning will be always the same: it is almost a geometrical problem: I have such a man, such a woman, in such surroundings. What can happen to them to oblige them to go to their limit? That's the question. It will be sometimes a very simple incident, anything which will change their lives. Then I write my novel chapter by chapter. I know nothing about the events when I begin the novel. On the envelope I put only the names of their characters, their ages, their families. I know nothing whatsoever about the events that will occur later. Otherwise it would not be interesting to me. On the eve of the first day I know what will happen in the first chapter. Then, day after day, chapter after chapter, I find what comes later. After I have started a novel I write a chapter each day, without ever missing a day. Because it is a strain, I have to keep pace with the novel. If, for example, I am ill for forty-eight hours, I have to throw away the previous chapters. And I never return to that novel. When I am doing a novel now I don't see anybody, I don't speak to anybody, I don't take a phone call, I live like a monk. All the day I am one of my characters. I feel what he feels. Most of my novels show what happens around one character. The other characters are always seen by him. So it is in this character's skin I have to be. And it's almost unbearable after five or six days. That is one of the reasons my novels are so short. Generally a few days before the start of a novel, I look to see that I don't have any appointments for eleven days. Then I call the doctor. He takes my blood pressure, he checks everything. And he says 'Okay'. Because I have to be sure that I am good for eleven days.'

It is also worth noting that before starting work, Simenon used to fill a rack full of pipes. Food was placed in an ante room at regular intervals during the eleven days it took him to write a book. Simenon would collect the tray, eat, and put the empty tray back in the ante room to be collected.

Carmen
Carmen is the most commonly produced opera of all time but when it was first produced, in 1875 in Paris, it was attacked – partly because audiences didn't like the fact that the heroine died at the end. A decade later the opera still attracted serious criticism and very little affection. The sadness is that it wasn't only Carmen who died too soon. Bizet, the composer, died of a broken heart at the age of 36, believing that his work was a failure.

Money
The money required to provide adequate food, water, education, health care and housing for everyone in the world is about the same as the world spends on arms every two weeks.

Duty
'In my humble opinion, non-cooperation with evil is as much a duty as is cooperation with good.' – *Mahatma Gandhi*

Free children
'They ought to give away a ten-year-old child with every video machine. And every other sort of machine they're swamping us with these days.' – *Gavin Lyall (Lyall's books about spies and the hinterland are infinitely better written than those of ex-spy John Le Carre – who for inexplicable reasons was incredibly popular with critics and film makers.)*

Mystery
After I had taken Antoinette home after her operation, I mentioned that I had suddenly started to shiver when I was in the chapel.

'What time was that?' she asked.

'About a quarter to twelve.'

Antoinette told me that at that time she'd been on the trolley in the recovery room and that she'd suddenly had a vicious attack of shivering – a response to the anaesthetic. You can argue it was a coincidence. But you can argue that it wasn't.

Alasdair Gray's Joke

When Alasdair Gray's book 'Unlikely Stories, Mostly' was first published in 1983, Mr Gray persuaded the publishers to inset a small slip of paper which was printed in red and which read:

ERRATUM

This slip has been inserted by mistake.

(I once saw a metal sign on a beach in North Devon which said only: 'Do Not Throw Stones at This Notice'. The sign, which stood alone and carried no other instruction, was peppered with rusting dents where it had been scarred by stones.)

Publishers with Red Faces

The following bestselling books were rejected by numerous (now presumably embarrassed and poorer) publishers.

Animal Farm – George Orwell
Dubliners – James Joyce
Lorna Doone – R.D.Blackmore
M*A*S*H – Richard Hooker
Northanger Abbey – Jane Austen
Jonathan Livingstone Seagull – Richard Bach
Harry Potter and the Philosopher's Stone – J.K.Rowling

Why?

The best, simplest and least asked question in the world is 'Why?' Why do you want a better job? Why do you want to save money?

Why do you want to move house? Only when you ask yourself Why? will you know what you really need and what you are prepared to do for it. Most people earn and spend without ever asking themselves Why? They blindly sell their time (which is the same as selling their lives) for money which they spend on things they neither want nor need. Ask yourself Why? more often and you will learn more about yourself.

Essential Vulnerability

Heroes all need an essence of vulnerability – a major threat to their existence and comfort. So, for example, Superman would be dull without the ever present threat of kryptonite, Sherlock Holmes would have had a dull existence but for Professor Moriarty and what would have been the point of James Bond without Ernst Stavros Blofeld?

Anarchy

'All men are anarchists at heart, or, if they are not, they should be ashamed of themselves. To one and all of us, at some time or other, amid technocratic pressures and totalitarian intimations, must come the urge to kick over the orthodox traces, to say insultingly what we think, to reduce authority to the shambles it deserves.' – *Michael Foot*

'Into the Silence' by Wade Davis

'Into the Silence' is a powerful, moving and highly recommended book which deals both with the Great War and the conquest of Mount Everest – using George Mallory and the other climbers as the link. Mallory and Sandy Irvine were, of course, the first men to climb Everest, and their final expedition consisted largely of men who had survived the dangers and privations of First World War. The book, a monumental tribute to the best men of a generation, tells their story. Wade Davis describes how, at the outbreak (of the Great War) a man had to stand five foot eight to join up but by November 1914, those as short as five-three were eagerly recruited. Many of the men who joined had signed up together, drawn by Kitchener's promise that those who enlisted together would fight together. They were intensely patriotic and shared a sense of duty and honour difficult to imagine today. In the trenches, each soldier would carry in addition to rifle and bayonet, sixty-six pounds of gear: wire cutters, 220 rounds of ammunition, mess kits, empty sandbags, flares, an entrenching shovel, battle dressings, two gas masks, and two grenades. How they stood up, let alone moved, is a mystery. Tragically, the men were let down by their leaders. So, for example, the woefully unimaginative General Haig always attacked at 7.30 in the morning. The Germans, of course, had their breakfast at 6.30 am and were sitting waiting.

Here are some quotes from Wade Davis's book:

Dr Tom Longstaff, medical officer on the 1922 Everest expedition said: 'I want to make one thing clear. I am the expedition's official medical officer. I am, as a matter of fact, a qualified doctor, but I feel it my duty now to remind you that I have never practised in my life. I beg you in no circumstances to seek my professional advice, since it would almost certainly turn out to be wrong. I am however willing if necessary to sign a certificate of death.'

The supplies for the 1922 Everest expedition included 'such delicacies as gingered lemons and tinned quail in aspic, not to mention a case of the finest French champagne and several bottles of 120-year-old rum.'

Finally, Wade Davis discusses whether George Mallory and Sandy Irvine reached the top of Everest. '…surely nothing could have held Mallory back. He would have walked on, even to his end, because for him, as for all of his generation, death was but 'a frail barrier' that men crossed, 'smiling and gallant every day'. 'They had seen so much of death that life mattered less than the moments of being alive.'

The Past Is No Longer There

For several years I intended to go back to visit the towns in English Midlands where I was born, went to school, attended medical school and eventually practised as a GP. But somehow I never got round to going back and when I eventually looked at satellite maps on the internet, I saw that everywhere I once knew had changed beyond recognition. There can be no going back to look at the school I attended and no way to retrace my journey to the public library I visited every Saturday morning. It would have been interesting to visit to see if the book shop, delicatessen, pharmacy, draper, barber, men's outfitter, tailor, antique shop and junk shop which I knew as a boy were still there but I'm confident that they have all gone. How can I be so sure? The streets have gone. Nothing is the same. Whole areas seem to have been demolished and rebuilt.

Second Hand

It sometimes seems that half the adults in the world lead their lives second hand through their parents ('My father is Lord Tweedledee; he's chairman of Rancid Plastics.') and the other half lead their lives second hand through their children ('My Elspeth is Junior Girls Tennis Champion for Southern Texas. After her seventh birthday we're entering her for Wimbledon. Her coach says she's the best six-year-old tennis player he's seen since last year.')

Dread

'I have a new philosophy. I'm only going to dread one day at a time.' – *Charles M.Schultz*

Microbes

'The microbe is nothing, the soil is everything.' – *Louis Pasteur*

Best War Movies
Where Eagles Dare
The Great Escape
M*A*S*H

Fantasies
Cherish your youthful fantasies and enjoy them to the full. In a few years' time all your waking hours will be spent worrying about mortgage rates, blocked drains and shingles.

Guests
'You must come again when you have less time.' – *Walter Sickert*

Zombie Pharm by Larry Beinhart
'No actual teachers were eaten during the writing of this book. Parts of this book were written under the influence of Adderall, some sections were inspired by hydrocodone. Reading this book may cause insomnia, nausea, weakness, headache, diarrhoea, anxiety, nervousness, tremor, incessant giggling, dry mouth, sweating, impotence, premature ejaculation, flushing and abnormal dreams. Eating this book may result in constipation, gas, vomiting hypertension, high blood pressure, weight gain, hostility or aggressiveness, restlessness, restless leg syndrome, ringing in the ears, memory loss, serotonin syndrome, chest palpitations, depression and suicidal thoughts. While rare, other side effects of reading may include, seizures, coma and death, in case of death immediately call your physician. These side effects should no more deter you from reading this book than from taking your medication.'

Bad Old Days

Sadly, I don't think the GP service has a future at all. In the old days, GPs used to give injections, take bloods, take smears, syringe ears, weigh people, provide dietary advice, sew wounds, take stitches out – all these are now handed over to nurses. GPs used to visit patients who had come from a hospital stay. I used to find considerable satisfaction in performing these simple tasks and I am certain that doing so helped cement the bond between doctor and patient. Today, GPs work library hours and do very little work. They aren't available at night or at weekends or on bank holidays. They never seem to visit patients at home. The idea that they offer support to their patients (in the traditional sense) is a joke – and a sick one at that. It annoys me enormously that they still seem to think they are providing a valuable service. Outside library hours there is no chance of talking to a doctor. We can either ring a 16-year-old on the NHS phone line (if it is still running) or call for an ambulance. Small, local hospitals have been shut or turned into office space for under-employed NHS staff and half empty day care centres for patients needing a little physiotherapy. Even inside the library hours there is little chance of seeing a GP without a long wait. Actually I don't know why I describe the GP as operating library hours. Most doctors' surgeries are shut at lunchtime but libraries are open during lunchtimes. So it's easier to borrow a book than it is to see a doctor.

Cricket in Hollywood

Hollywood stars C.Aubrey Smith and Nigel Bruce (known as Willie to his friends) were cricket fanatics – rather like the two gentlemen in 'The Lady Vanishes'. Bruce was the best wicket keeper in America and Smith had played for Sussex and had captained England at cricket. Smith had it written into his contracts that if he had to make a picture in England he would not be obliged to work on days when Test Matches were being played. (Trevor Howard was reported to have done the same.) Smith was famous in Hollywood for distrusting the American press. He relied entirely upon the

London Times for his news and since the paper took five days to arrive this often caused confusion when he discussed international affairs with colleagues. (He was five days late realising that the Second World War had begun.) Smith only gave up playing cricket when he reached the age of 80. He was ordered to stop by Nigel Bruce and Boris Karloff who feared that the former England captain would have a heart attack and drop dead.

Colonel Bruce

Charles Bruce, a British soldier, was said to be so strong that he could, with his arms extended, lift a grown man seated in a chair off the ground to the level of his ears. To keep fit, Colonel Bruce regularly ran up and down the flanks of the Khyber Pass carrying his orderly on his back. As a middle-aged colonel he would wrestle six of his men at once. His sporting activities weren't limited to outdoor displays. It was said by some that he had slept with the wife of every enlisted man in the force.

David Niven's War

When World War II started, actor David Niven was desperate to rush back to England to join the army. But Niven was under contract to Sam Goldwyn and was shooting a film entitled 'Raffles' at the time. Niven's request to be released from the film was refused, and so he persuaded a friend in England to send a phony cable reading: 'Report to Depot immediately'. When Goldwyn checked and found that Niven had arranged for the cable to be sent, he threatened to sue. When Niven was eventually released, Goldwyn told Niven: 'I am cabling Hitler to ask him to shoot all round you.'

Famous English stars in Hollywood

The early years of Hollywood were dominated by British actors. Here's a list (in no particular order) of just some of the British stars

who shone brightly on the silver screen:
Richard Burton
George Sanders
Peter Ustinov
Charlie Chaplin
Noel Coward
James Mason
Ray Milland
Cary Grant
C Aubrey Smith
Nigel Bruce
Ronald Colman
George Arliss
David Niven
Leslie Howard
Boris Karloff
Cedric Hardwicke
Richard Greene
Basil Rathbone
Herbert Marshall
Laurence Olivier
Charles Laughton
Cary Grant
Robert Newton
James Mason
Stewart Granger
Anthony Steel
Rex Harrison
Jean Simmons
Robert Donat
Greer Garson
Deborah Kerr
Ida Lupino
Gladys Cooper
Joan Fontaine
Olivia de Havilland
Vivien Leigh

Death
In 1914, the chances of a British boy aged between 13 and 24 surviving the war were one in three. Put another way, two out of three would die. Nancy Cooper claimed that by the end of 1916, every boy she had ever danced with was dead. Had each man who died in the war been granted one page upon which to write his life story the result would have been a library of 26,000 books, with each book being 600 pages long.

He didn't mean it
'This suspense is terrible – I hope it will last.' – *Oscar Wilde*

Crooks
Never trust anyone who offers to look after your money or give you advice. Lest you think this unduly sceptical, let me remind you that in 2023, the Financial Conduct Authority in the UK revealed that many investment firms were not only keeping the interest paid on their clients' accounts but were also charging fees for doing so. In practice, this means that if a customer had £1,000 in cash with an investment or pension company then the company would retain the interest paid on the £1,000 while, at the same time, charging the customer a chunky fee for providing the account. I repeat: never trust anyone who offers to look after your money or give you advice.

Politeness
The glass partitions in shops, banks and post offices all carry large signs insisting that customers must always be polite, considerate, respectful, grateful and deferential. Customers are told that they must not ask difficult questions. What a pity it is that copies of these signs are not hung on the other side of the glass partitions.

The Internet
Anything which you post on the internet will remain there forever and will become public property the minute it is posted.

Nuts
'I couldn't take all those nut cases any more. You'd think once in a while somebody would notice that I have problems too.' – *Psychiatrist who shot a woman patient who kept complaining*

Bodypower
Bodypower was my first international bestselling book. First published in 1983, it was a *Sunday Times* bestseller and it was published around the world. Numerous TV shows and radio programmes were made about it, and the book itself was serialised for weeks in a number of the world's leading newspapers and magazines. Bodypower changed my life – not because it was successful but because it enabled me to share my thoughts about the body's self-healing powers.

The book began in the autumn of 1980

I was in Vienna and the weather was freezing cold. Outside in the street the wind cut through my thin raincoat as if it wasn't there. I walked with my shoulders hunched and my hands stuffed deep inside my coat pockets. My fingers felt numb. I was so cold that I could hardly think; even my brain felt frozen. I was shivering involuntarily and uncontrollably.

It was dusk. The skies were dark with rain to come, and in the early evening gloom the bright lights of the cafe seemed especially warm and promising. I love the cafes of Vienna and Paris. They remind me of the sort of places where Dr Johnson might have talked with friends in London a couple of centuries ago. Through the open curtains I could see the dark wooden tables and chairs, the racks of newspapers neatly folded around wooden sticks and the plump, bosomy Austrian waitress hurrying about with vast cups of cream-topped coffee.

I went in, found a table near to the window and sat down. Inside the cafe it was cosy and comfortable. Old-fashioned radiators and a log stove gurgled pleasantly and the air smelt of ground coffee beans and rich chocolate cake. The waitress approached and smiled at me. I gave her my order, took my hands out of my pockets and tried to rub them together. They were white with cold and I could hardly move my fingers. I cupped my hands, held them up to my face and blew on them. Slowly the feeling came back into them. Slowly the colour returned. Gingerly I flexed and extended my fingers; gradually I regained the movement I had lost. As I watched my frozen fingers changing colour, I suddenly became aware of something that was to change my life. I suddenly became conscious of the remarkable powers of the human body to adapt itself to cope with its environment. Outside in the bitterly cold autumn air the blood had left my fingers to reduce the amount of heat lost in order to try to maintain my internal body temperature. My body had been prepared to sacrifice my fingers to save itself. Inside, in the warmth of the cafe, the blood had rushed back into my hands. Once my body's internal thermometer had recognised that the temperature inside the cafe was warm, my body no longer had to fight to keep me alive. I felt the shivering stop and slipped off my coat. I picked up the coffee which the waitress had brought me and held my head in the steam rising from it.

Sitting in that cafe in Vienna, with my thawing hands wrapped around a steaming cup of coffee, I realized that the human body has far more extensive, protective and self-healing powers than we give it credit for. I realized that all of us, doctors and patients, tend to be too quick to rush for the medicine cabinet when things go wrong.

I took out my notebook and pencil (for years I have never gone anywhere without both) and immediately wrote down the outline for a book I knew I wanted to write. I wanted to try to teach doctors as well as patients that the human body has far-reaching powers that we ignore far too often. I wanted to try to persuade patients to learn to listen to their own bodies and to avoid interfering with their bodies unless absolutely necessary. I wanted to teach doctors that they should not always assume that whenever illness strikes intervention is essential. I wanted to show both patients and doctors that we all underestimate the remarkable healing powers of the human body.

The truth is that most illnesses are not serious but are treated as if they are. And so I wrote 'Bodypower' explaining the remarkable self-healing powers of the human body and showing exactly how those powers could be harnessed.

The philosophy I described in Bodypower changed my life, and has influenced everything I've written about medicine since 1980. It has also influenced hundreds of medical writers, thousands of doctors and millions of patients. The Bodypower philosophy is now widely acknowledged and accepted. In 1983 the philosophy behind Bodypower seemed new and slightly frightening to many people. I'm pleased to say that today the philosophy described in Bodypower is widely accepted.

Babylon

In Babylonia, people used to carry sick relatives or friends to the city square, and lay or sit them down in full view of those passing by. The passers-by were expected to ask what was wrong and to share advice and experience. Now that there is very little health care left, maybe it is time to resurrect the practice.

Old Age

'Old age is always 15 years older than I am.' – *Bernard Baruch*

Speechless

'I was literally speechless,' he said. – *(Report in a magazine)*

Playing Nurse

If little girls want to play nurse they should just sit somewhere quiet and eat chocolates and biscuits. That's all nurses seem to do these days.

Testing Students

Medical students and nursing students and all students in any health care speciality should, at some time in their training, be examined and a diagnostic test of some kind done. And then they should be told that they might have something seriously wrong with them. But that they will be given their results in a month's time. And then they would learn.

Thieves

I was looking for a novel by P.G.Wodehouse today. Within minutes I found a dozen different versions of the book I wanted. It was clear that most of the books were pirated copies. (Wodehouse died on St Valentine's Day in 1975 and so his books will remain in copyright until St Valentine's Day in 2045.) There are, it seems, a growing number of people who regard copyright theft as a victimless crime. It isn't. There are on the internet at the moment at least three books which contain nothing but articles which appeared on my website. And the contents of at least two books of mine which appeared as paperbacks and eBooks have been stolen and published under other names on the internet. No one will do anything about this copyright theft which is more common than is widely realised and which will, it seems, be exacerbated as AI becomes more popular.

Ageing

It is a curiously levelling thought (cheering to any older citizen who has been patronised by someone far younger than themselves) that anyone over the age of 20 is already deteriorating. And anyone over the age of 35 is already well on their way down the steep, downward and slippery slope to oblivion: brain cells are dying, muscles are getting weaker, bones are collapsing, organs are deteriorating. There, I feel better already.

Pigeons

Pigeons learn quickly and have long memories. When we lived in Paris we defied the police and the locals by feeding the pigeons on our window sill. Even after we had been away for weeks, the pigeons would tap at the window, tap their feet on the lead windowsill outside and peer expectantly into the apartment the moment the shutters were raised and a light switched on. The pigeons never bothered to do this at the windows where they had not been fed.

Questions

Questions are more powerful than statements (and often legally safer). I don't know why this should be the case, but it is. So, if a newspaper headline asks: 'Is Donald Trump insane?' the paper will attract more readers than if the headline merely states: 'Donald Trump is insane'. Similarly, 'Is Boris Johnson a psychopath?' is stronger than the bald 'Boris Johnson is a psychopath.'

Sports Invented By the English

The English no longer lead the world in sports, as they once did. But the English can at least claim to have invented more sports than any other nation. Here, in no particular order, and not including tiddlywinks, is a list of some of the sports the English gave the world.
Football (Association) a.k.a. soccer
Football (Rugby)
Cricket
Bowling

Hockey
Ice hockey
Snooker
Skiing
Tobogganing
Sailing
Boxing
Darts
Archery
Motor racing
Billiards
Skittles (modernised as Ten Pin Bowling)
Rounders (which became baseball)
Table tennis
Netball (which became basketball)
Squash

Rules

'If you obey all the rules, you miss all the fun.' – *Katherine Hepburn*

Young achievers

The high achiever who becomes a manager of a fast food restaurant at 24 years of age should know that:
Mozart wrote his first symphony at 8
William Pitt the Younger was Prime Minister of England at 24
Hannibal – led an army across the Alps at 26
Alexander the Great - conquered Greece and India and created a great empire at the age of 18
Augustus Caesar – was a Roman Senator at 20
Joan of Arc was 17 when she had a commanding role in the French army
Blaise Pascal was 19 when he developed the first calculator
Mary Shelley was 20 when she wrote and published the novel 'Frankenstein'

Galusha Pennypacker was 21 when he was appointed a brigadier general in the Union Army in the American Civil War. Lawrence Bragg won the Nobel Prize in Physics at 25

Thoughts on Health

'Look to your health: and if you have it, praise God, and value it next to a good conscience; for health is the second blessing that we mortals are capable of; a blessing that money cannot buy.' – *Izaak Walton*

'Doctors are always working to preserve our health and cooks to destroy it, but the latter are the more often successful.' – *Denis Diderot*

'Strive to preserve your health; and in this you will the better succeed in proportion as you keep clear of the physicians, for their drugs are a kind of alchemy concerning which there are no fewer books than there are medicines.' – *Leonardo da Vinci*

'...no road that would lead us to health is either arduous or expensive.' – *Michel de Montaigne*

'To preserve one's health by too strict a regime is in itself a tedious malady.' – *Duc Francois de La Rochefoucauld*

'Your body knows best. Learn to listen to it.' – *Vernon Coleman*

Tolkien to his Publisher

'I am well aware that 'dwarfs' is the correct modern English plural of dwarf; but I intend to use 'dwarves' for good reasons of my own. I take it harder that my 'elven'… should be replaced, though not consistently, by the detestable Spenserian 'elfin', which it was specially designed to avoid. I never have voluntarily used, and do not intend (if I can avoid it) to be represented as using the form 'farther' for the older 'further', and should be grateful if the 'further' of my copy could be left alone. I think it would be much better, and save time and annoyance in the end, if it was assumed that all apparent oddities and idiosyncrasies were intentional.'

The above is an extract from a letter from J.R.R.Tolkein to his publisher Allen & Unwin, London on July 22, 1953, as the first part of the Lord of the Rings trilogy ('The Fellowship of the Ring') was prepared for publication.

Hitler Whoopsie

In 1983, the *Sunday Times* reported the discovery of 60 volumes of Hitler's diaries, which had been acquired by the German magazine *Stern* for £2,460,000 after being found in a hayloft. A distinguished historian, Professor Hugh Trevor-Roper (also known as Lord Dacre) vouched for the authenticity. There was much egg on a number of faces when a chemical expert proved that the paper used for the diaries wasn't in use until after Hitler's death. A Stuttgart dealer in military relics called Konrad Kujau (aka Peter Fischer) confessed to forgery and was given a four year prison sentence.

Work

'Much of the world's work is done by men who do not feel quite well.' – *J.K.Galbraith*

Dunwich – The Town Lost at Sea

The village of Dunwich was the capital of East Anglia during the Roman occupation of England. By the mid-1800s, Dunwich had shrunk and had a population of just over 200. Curiously, it was, however, allowed to return two MPs to Parliament. But storms and high seas gradually overcame the village, and a total of eight churches and hundreds of smaller buildings disappeared.

Dunwich is just one of many English towns which have disappeared. Other lost towns include Withernsea, Hardburn, Frismarch, Dymitton, Outnewton, Hotten, Northorpe, Hornsea Burton and Old Kilham. Many of these have been lost to erosion. In Yorkshire it has for centuries been common for a hundred feet of coast to disappear in a single year. Coastal erosion is promoted as a new phenomenon but it patently isn't.

Billiards and Bar Billiards

Billiards is a far more accessible game than snooker. It is possible for a beginner to amass a comparatively massive score with very little practice. For those with insufficient space for a billiard table, I recommend bar billiards – a game which was once popular in public houses but which has now been pushed out of the way by gaming machines. Bar billiard tables cost relatively little and can be fitted into a corner of a modest sized room.

Palmerston

Lord Palmerston, a former British Prime Minister died of a heart attack in 1865 while having sex with a maid on his billiard table. Palmerston was two days away from his 81st birthday. He was Prime Minister twice, for a total of nine years.

Bravery

People were much braver back in the distant days of the 20th century. They stuck up for themselves and wouldn't take any nonsense from those in authority. Today, oddly, most people are ruder and nastier to one another but exceedingly compliant when faced with bureaucracy.

Over 75

At least a third of all cancers occur in people who are 75 or older.

Education
'The best part of every man's education, is that which he gives to himself.' – *Walter Scott*

Talking
'We don't hold much with talking to patients in this ward.' – *Nurse in NHS hospital*

Reviewers
A growing number of reviewers review the book they'd like to have read, rather than the book the author has written.

Babe
When the film Babe (about a talking piglet) was shown in Hong Kong, the title was changed to 'The Happy Dumpling-To-Be who Talks and solves Agricultural Problems'. Not quite as snappy, perhaps but presumably well suited to the local market.

Cheque mate
When I was a GP I drove a Mini Countryman which I had bought from my mother, so I know it had one careful lady owner (it was one of the Minis with wood on the sides). On my afternoon off, I drove to Edgbaston in Birmingham to watch a county cricket match. Unfortunately, on the way there a van hit the side of the car and caused considerable damage. A local garage did the repairs and took some weeks over it. I took a taxi to the garage to pick up the car and when I got there, the garage owner refused to let me take the car away unless I paid by a bank transfer. (As usual the van's insurers had only paid for part of the damage) I wanted to give him a cheque,

which would save me calling another taxi to take me to a bank. The garage owner was adamant. And then I had a brainwave (one of those ideas which usually come a day too late). 'Before we do anything else I need a test drive,' I said. The garage owner agreed. We got in the car and drove around for ten minutes before I pulled into the kerb about a mile from the garage. I took out my cheque book and wrote him a cheque. 'You can either accept the cheque or I'll drive you back to Leamington Spa and go to my bank. You can then find your own way back to Birmingham.' He took the cheque.

Polls

In 2024, a large poll showed that 54% of American college students believe that students should be exposed to all kinds of speech even if they may find it offends them in some way. The other 46% believe that anyone who says anything with which they disagree should be banned from their college. In 2016, the figure allowing freedom of speech was a rather more healthy (but still disappointing) 78%.

Toxins

Back in 2600 BC, the doctors looking after an Egyptian pharaoh called Imhotep deliberately encouraged a localised infection in order to cause a tumour to regress. In the 13th century, St Peregrine had a tumour which disappeared after it became infected. A couple of centuries ago, it was standard treatment to infect tumours in order to destroy them. Anton Chekhov, the Russian author, noticed that the infection erysipelas encouraged the remission of a cancer. Using infection to kill a cancer was given a more solid scientific basis by William Coley, an oncologist working at the Hospital for Special Surgery in the USA. After some mixed results in 1893, Coley began work with streptococcus pyogenes and serratia marcescens and published his results as a series of case studies.

The theory behind Coley's Toxins is based upon the fact that the body's defence cells, macrophages, do not recognise cancer as an enemy. Cancer cells and tissues are seen as normal body tissue. By simulating an infection at the site of a cancer tumour, the body will create a fever and encourage higher activity of the immune system. From 1893 until 1963, the Coley's Toxins were widely used against a variety of different types of cancer. One of the big drug companies, Parke-Davis, marketed the product with some success. However, in 1962, after the Kefauver Harris Amendment was passed in the USA, Coley's Toxins were given 'new drug' status by the Food and Drug Administration and it became illegal to prescribe the treatment other than within a clinical trial. In Europe, Coley's Toxins were made by a small German drug company until 1990 when official production was stopped by the German authorities. (In Germany, there was a loophole in the law. Doctors are allowed to produce unapproved treatments as long as they don't sell them or give them away. And so the law allowed doctors to prepare Coley's toxins and to use them if and when they thought the treatment appropriate.) In other parts of the world the principle of using an infection to encourage a cure is still accepted. An American friend of ours, who currently lives in Thailand, developed cancer of the bladder. He was treated, most successfully, by having tuberculosis injected into his bladder at the site of the cancer. In the West he would be said to have been cured. Today, there is still no official evidence that Coley's Toxins cure cancer and, sadly, there are, as far as I know, no big clinical trials being conducted or planned. As usual, the problem seems to be that drug companies (who conduct or control almost all medical research and who control many of the cancer charities and the cancer industry) see little or no profit in Coley's Toxins, although it isn't difficult to argue that the Toxins are more effective and certainly a lot less dangerous than some of the incredibly expensive chemotherapy products on the market.

Destroyed
'I have known more men destroyed by the desire to have a wife and child and to keep them in comfort than I have seen destroyed by drink and harlots.' – *W.B.Yeats*

Great English Inventors

The English have invented far more good and useful stuff than any other nationality. Unfortunately, they rarely seem to have succeeded in making a profit out of their inventions. Here's a short list of some English inventors:

Charles Babbage (computer – without which IBM, Microsoft, Apple, etc., would not exist)

John Baskerville (type – without which monks would still be writing out books by hand)

Roger Bacon (magnifying glasses, spectacles, telescopes, gunpowder and flying machines – leaving very little for anyone else to invent)

Richard Arkwright (spinning frame – which helped revolutionise the clothing industry in particular and factory work in general)

John Fleming (vacuum diode – a fundamental item in any electrical circuit)

William Henry Fox Talbot (photography – without which the egotists would have to draw their selfies)

Robert Hooke (universal joint which connects straight things and lets them go round bends)

Frank Whittle (jet propulsion – without which it would take a lot longer to get anywhere)

William Henry Perkin (synthetic dyes, without which we'd have to rely on woad)

Michael Faraday (dynamo – without which electricity wouldn't happen)

Edmund Halley (diving bell – without which the depths of the sea would remain unexplored)

Earl of Sandwich (sandwich without which picnics would be far less practical and office workers would have messier desks)

Thomas Saint (sewing machine, without which it would take seven months to make a pair of trousers)

John Walker (friction match, without which fire lighting would require a boy scout, a magnifying glass and a bunch of straw)

Rowland Hill (postage stamp, without which there would be no mail)

Isaac Newton (the law of gravity, without which the apple would probably still be on the tree)

Joseph Bramah (the hydraulic press without which nothing would be flat)
Francis Pettit Smith (the propeller, without which boats and aeroplanes would never move far)
George Stephenson (the first locomotive without which the 5.46 from Paddington would still be standing at Platform 3 and several hundred commuters would be cursing)
Christopher Cockerell (the hovercraft without which explorers would take twice as long to cross swampy ground)
Joseph Lister (antiseptic surgery which revolutionised surgery and has saved millions of lives)
Edwin Budding (the lawnmower which enabled gardeners to give their lawns lovely looking stripes)
Tim Berners-Lee (the World Wide Web, though I'm not sure this counts as a 'good thing' for without the WWW there would be no Google, no Facebook and no social media – and, so, no, Berners-Lee must go to the back of the class)

Cats

The Spanish don't like cats very much and often treat them very poorly. In the past Spaniards have eaten cats or turned them into rugs. The Spanish once had a Minister in Tangier who turned the Moroccan nation against him. He killed a couple of battalions of cats and had a carpet made out of their skins. He made the carpet in circles, with a circle of old grey tom cats, with their tails all pointing towards the centre, then a circle of yellow cats, then a circle of black cats, then a circle of white ones, then a circle of all sorts of cats, and finally a centrepiece of assorted kittens. The Moors, who like cats, cursed him for years.

Political history

Political history can be very confusing. Historians say that UK Prime Minister Margaret Thatcher was defeated by her unpopular poll tax. But the poll tax (a logical and fair replacement for local taxes on homes) was only unpopular with a small but noisy group of scroungers and layabouts. Large families (who require more council services) didn't like the idea because it would mean that their tax bills would rise according to the number of adults living in a property. Ordinary taxpayers, whose bills would remain much the same, thought that the poll tax was sensible, and it was understood that it would benefit elderly widows and widowers living alone. But a few relatively modest demonstrations and near riots and left wing media opposition meant that the poll tax was replaced with a council tax based on property values – a nonsense, of course, since it is individuals not properties which require roads, schools and other council services. The history of Thatcher's demise illustrates the power a small mob can wield and the ability of left wing historians to rewrite history.

Animal rights

'I am in favour of animal rights as well as human rights. That is the way of a whole human being.' – *Abraham Lincoln*

Types of Auctions

Ordinary English auction. The auctioneer invites bids and the bidders push up the prices bit by bit.

A Dutch auction works. This works in reverse. The auctioneer starts at a high price and the price falls until a bidder says he'll pay that price. It's a pity there aren't more of these.

Paper or silent auction. Auction announces a minimum price and the bidders write down their bids and the highest wins.

Ring auction. Dealers agree not to bid. One of them buys the item. They then all meet and have the auction between themselves.

Market auction. Bidders bid on a bunch of similar items and can take as many as they like at that price.

Time auction. The bidding stops at a pre-arranged time. Time auctions can be pretty chaotic. The French have a version which they use when selling wine. The auctioneer lights a candle and people can bid for as long as the candle remains alight – though every bid must be higher than the last one. When the candle goes out the last bid gets the item.

Obscenity
'Obscene is not the picture of a naked woman exposed but that of a fully-clad general who exposes his medals won in a war of aggression.' – *Herbert Marcuse*

Gardens
'Today, gardening is the most revolutionary act there is.' – *Vandana Shiva*

A Dozen Traditional English pastimes for children
All these pastimes are now considered unsafe or are banned for one reason or another. Health and safety officials would much rather children stayed indoors watching television or playing with their smart phones.
1. Conkers
2. Bowling a hoop
3. Light a fire with a magnifying glass
4. Skimming flat stones over water
5 Play pooh sticks on a stream
6. Climbing a tree
7. Looking in rock pools
8. Building a sandcastle on a beach
9. Whittling a stick with a penknife
10. Making a daisy chain
11. Making and using a bow and arrow
12. Collect driftwood/shells, etc., on beach

Names
'Everyone has a right to pronounce foreign names as he chooses.' – *Winston Churchill*

England in the early 19th century
'In the morning all is calm – not a mouse stirring before ten o'clock; the shops then begin to open. Milk-women, with their pails perfectly neat, suspended at the two extremities of a yoke, carefully shaped to fit the shoulders, and surrounded with small tin measures of cream, ring at every door, with reiterated pulls, to hasten the maid servants, who come half asleep to receive a measure as big as an egg, being the allowance of a family; for it is necessary to explain, that milk is not here either food or drink, but a tincture – an elixir exhibited in drops, five or six at most, in a cup of tea, morning an evening. It would be difficult to say what taste or what quality these drops may impart; but so it is; and nobody thinks of questioning the propriety of the custom.' – *From 'An American in Regency England: The Journal of a Tour in 1810-1811' by Louis Simond*

More about England in the Early 19th Century
'Politics are a subject of such general interest in England, both for men and women, that it engrosses the conversation before, as much as after the retreat of the ladies; the latter, indeed, are still more violent and extravagant than the men, whenever they meddle at all with politics, and the men out of Parliament, I think, more than those in Parliament. Women, however, do not speak much in numerous and mixed company. Towards the end of dinner, and before the ladies retire, bowls of coloured glass, full of water are placed before each person. All (women as well as men) stoop over it, sucking up some of the water, and returning it, often more than once, and with a spitting and washing sort of noise, quite charming – the operation

frequently assisted by a finger elegantly thrust into the mouth! This, however, is nothing to what I am going to relate. Drinking much and long leads to unavoidable consequences. Will it be credited, that, in a corner of the very dining room, there is a certain convenient piece of furniture to be used by anybody who wants it. The operation is performed very deliberately and un-disguisedly, as a matter of course, and occasions no interruption of the conversation.' – *Also from 'An American in Regency England: The Journal of a Tour in 1810-1811' by Louis Simond*

Crime

I have come to realise that the greatest crime of our age is to question the deceits, misinformation and disinformation disseminated by the institutions which have assumed authority over our existence. Truth is no excuse these days. After I had exposed the covid fraud (proving beyond doubt that the so-called pandemic was nothing more than a standard annual flu with better marketing) and explained why the covid-19 vaccine was useless and toxic, I was roundly condemned by a wide variety of institutions. Google libelled me, YouTube banned me and the mainstream media abused me, censored me, suppressed me and demonised me. They all refused to debate or discuss. But the most surprising thing that happened was when the Royal Society of Arts expelled me for the curious modern crime of telling the truth. I found it sad and rather pathetic that an institution with some history should bow to pressure in order to punish and outlaw someone whom they should have known had done nothing but tell the truth.

Rudeness

'It's curious how completely powerless almost all Englishmen are, if they're brought up against genuinely thorough rudeness. And in our absurd muddle-headed way we always estimate it as a sign of character. Dr Johnson and the Duke of Wellington and Queen Victoria and Mr Shaw and Mr Snowden – we find other reasons for approving of them, but actually we're just impressed by their sheer boorishness.' – *C.P.Snow*

Aristocracy
'The great distinction between the English aristocracy and any other has always been that, whereas abroad every member of a noble family is noble, in England none are noble except the head of the family. In spite of the fact that they enjoy courtesy titles, the sons and daughters of Lords are commoners – though not so common as baronets and their wives who take precedence after honourables.' – *Nancy Mitford*

Saying No
When you have difficulty saying No, think how much more difficult things are likely to become if you say Yes.

Too bad
'Too bad all the people who know how to run the country are busy driving taxicabs and cutting hair.' – *George Burns*

William Cobbett on Debt
'Nothing is so well calculated to produce a death-like torpor in the country as an extended system of taxation and a great national debt.' – *William Cobbett*

St Augustine
St Augustine once saw a child trying to empty the sea with a shell.

Every time I communicate with a utility company or government department I remember that child. Dealing with utility companies and government departments is a thankless, never ending business which I know will almost certainly get me nowhere.

Authority and Uniforms

'Whenever you give anyone any modicum of authority, especially if it comes with a uniform, they will always, always, abuse it.' – *Richard Littlejohn*

An MOT

On January 10th 2005, my father took his Skoda motor car to Pollitt Devon Daihatsu Centre in Exeter for an MOT. The car failed and my father had to drive the car back home, make a fresh appointment and then take the car back to be tested again. Naturally, there was another fee to pay. The garage gave just one reason for refusing a Test Certificate. Here it is: 'Offside lower windscreen has a sticker or other obstruction encroaching into the swept area by more than 40 mm outside zone A (8.3.1e).' The refusal form was signed by P.J.Spencer. The 'sticker or other obstruction' was actually my father's cardboard disabled parking badge which he had left visible, propped up against the windscreen. My father was 84-years-old at the time. I keep the form by my desk as a constant reminder of the world in which we now live. This is the sort of bizarre mentality which the system allows and expects. We all see examples of it every day. It is the world they have given us and too many people are prepared to do their bidding. In his final years my father was treated appallingly by his doctors (one of whom succeeded in killing him) and his dentist. It was, I think, the first time that I realised just how the elderly were being mistreated and abused by people who were being well paid to provide care for them.

The Bizarre Tale of Oliver Cromwell's Head

When Charles II was restored to the throne, out of revenge for signing his father's death warrant, he had Cromwell's body dug up from his resting place at Westminster Abbey. After being dug up from his resting place, Cromwell's corpse was taken to the Red Lion pub in Holburn. The next day the body was taken on a sledge through the streets of London to Tyburn. Cromwell's dead body was then hanged by the neck from the gallows for approximately six hours before being cut down and beheaded. It took the axe man eight blows to chop off his head. Cromwell's now headless body was then thrown into a lime-pit below the gallows at Tyburn. His head was displayed on a metal spike which was transfixed onto a 20-foot wooden pole. The pole stood on the roof of Westminster Hall. Cromwell's head was displayed on the pole for over 20 years. One night, a ferocious storm broke the spike causing Cromwell's head to fall. A sentinel who was on guard duty at the time was nearly hit by Cromwell's head as it landed with a thud by his feet. The soldier took the head home with him and put it up his chimney. On his deathbed, the soldier confessed to his daughter that he had placed Cromwell's head in the family chimney 20 years earlier. The family then sold the head, and in 1710 the head was seen in Du Puy's show of curiosities in London. In 1738, Du Puy died and the head wasn't seen again for approximately 40 years. An unsuccessful comic actor, Samuel Russell who claimed to be a descendant of Oliver Cromwell, then acquired the head. Having failed to sell the head to Cromwell's former college in Cambridge, he displayed Cromwell's head on a stall near the Clare Market in London. In 1787, London jeweller James Cox bought Cromwell's head for £118. Then, in 1799, the Hughes brothers bought the head from Cox for £230. They displayed it in a building in Bond Street. In 1815, Josiah Wilkinson of Kent, bought Cromwell's head from the Hughes family and kept it in a small box to show family, friends and curious visitors. And finally, in 1960, the Wilkinson family offered Cromwell's head to his former college in Cambridge so that it could finally be laid to rest. The college gladly accepted the head. Cromwell's head was buried in the grounds of the college on the 25th March 1960.

Careers
'All political careers…end in failure.' – *Enoch Powell*

Martin Sheen
Actor Martin Sheen, the actor who is famous for numerous film roles and who played President Jed Bartlett in TV series 'The West Wing', is also a political activist. He is reported to have been arrested 66 times for non-violent acts of civil disobedience. Henry David Thoreau would be proud of him.

Knowledge
The older I get and the more I learn, the less I seem to know.

Constable in Disgrace
'A curator at the National Gallery (in London) has rehung Constable's famous Suffolk painting 'The Hay Wain' and declared it 'a contested landscape'. Evidently the point of the painting shouldn't be what you see, and what has made it a great work of art, but what you don't see. The curator wants us to look at this remarkable painting, beloved by every country-man with critical disdain. To her mind, the important point is not its beauty, its brush strokes, its depiction of rural England, but to bemoan Constable's political incorrectness in not including in the landscape something to highlight the misery of many labouring lives. Horror of horrors, it appears that Constable himself was comfortably off and undeniably middle class, the son of a prosperous corn merchant and a man who 'upheld conservative values'. No wonder this is a 'contested landscape'! Clearly we have to contest anything or anyone who doesn't uphold such progressive doctrines. The quality of the painting is evidently immaterial. The only thing to do with this

pompous nonsense is to laugh. If the trustees of the National Gallery had a sense of proportion, they'd put up a notice saying: 'The notes to this exhibition are designed as an elaborate joke. Sensible people will just marvel at the wonderful paintings.' – *Country Life magazine (2024)*

Privacy
If a piece of paper (even an envelope) has your name and address on it (let alone any other details) you should burn it, rather than place it in a bin of any kind.

Expensive Bus Ride
In London, England, a man who was wrongly convicted of not paying his bus fare was initially fined a total of £776.50 – a £500 fine, the £1.50 fare, costs of £225 and a victim surcharge of £30.

Prime Minister
One in every four million Britons has been Prime Minister.

Smuggling
In the 18th century, and early 19th century smuggling was rife on the southern English coasts of Devon, Dorset and Cornwall. Huge numbers of revenue officers and customs officers were employed to stop the smugglers. But the revenue officers and customs officers knew that if they were successful in halting smuggling operations then their own jobs would be in jeopardy. There would obviously be no need to hire men to stop the smugglers if there were no smugglers. The smugglers and the customs men were symbiotic. This strange state of affairs is common in many areas of public life

today – with the malefactors and the governing agencies conspiring to defraud the public.

Puzzle
When did answering machines become known as voice mail? And why?

Ken Tynan – Conspiracy Theorist
'Inflation rides high, and I believe intentionally. A super-rich class is being built on top of the existing structure – an international-conglomerate-business rich, drawing on the US and the Common Market – with the aim of keeping the insurgent and overweening middle classes in their place, and of decisively depressing the proletariat (and restricting their aims to merely increasing their wages to keep pace with inflation). Only members of the super-rich – the new feudal class – will be able to keep their heads above the decline in the real value of money, because they are paid in perks, property, possessions and tax-exempt benefits. This is what will separate them from the rest of us, whose effects will perforce be dedicated not to changing society but to keeping ourselves from drowning. Thus cunningly manipulated, inflation can create (as well as destroy) a ruling class.' – *Kenneth Tynan (in 1973)*

My Favourite Novelists
1. Georges Simenon
2. Charles Dickens
3. Daniel Defoe
4. W Somerset Maugham
5. Jerome K Jerome
6. Jules Verne
7. C.S.Forester
8. Arnold Bennett

10. J.B. Priestley
11. George Orwell
12. Beverley Nichols
13. Evelyn Waugh
14. Ernest Hemingway
15. H.G. Wells
16. Paul Gallico
17. George Gissing
18. C.P. Snow
19. Victor Canning
20. Henry Fielding
21. P.G. Wodehouse
22. Sir Arthur Conan Doyle

Wallpaper

'My wallpaper and I are fighting a duel to the death. One or the other of us has to go.' – *Oscar Wilde*

Doctors off the Career Track

Today, doctors all determinedly follow a strict career path. From the moment they purchase their first stethoscope they take aim for a distant target with the dedicated aim of becoming a GP, an obstetrician, a forensic psychiatrist or an orthopaedic surgeon specialising in left knees. In the bad old days, there were students (and I confess I was one of them) who left medical school with one ambition remaining: never again to sit any examinations. It was these young doctors who provided ageing, single-handed GPs with locums, ships with the doctors they needed before they could set sail and casualty departments (the forerunners of Accident and Emergency Departments) with surgeons to stitch up accident victims on a Saturday night. Eventually, of course, most young doctors would settle down and step foot on a career path of some kind. But they would, I believe, be more rounded, more capable, more knowledgeable of the world, and better able to care for their patients, for having spent a year or two off the beaten track.

Litter, Kindling and Councils

Councils have made it illegal for anyone to pick up bits of wood from the roadside. Individuals who collected broken branches and kindling to take home to burn have been arrested and charged with theft by aggressive councils who have claimed ownership of fallen wood found on the roadside. Councils claim the rationale behind this oppressive, heavy handed behaviour is that our trees must all be protected because they eat up carbon dioxide and also because burning wood is bad for the environment. It is strange, therefore, that governments everywhere obtain much of their 'green' power by burning wood in power stations. Moreover, in the UK and Europe the wood comes from trees in America which are cut down and chopped up with petrol or diesel powered saws, transported to the East Coast in diesel powered lorries and trains and then carried across the Atlantic ocean on diesel powered ships before being taken from the ports to the power stations in diesel powered lorries. Despite the burning of all this fossil fuel, the official, government approved burning of wood is officially labelled 'green', and considered to be just as harmless and as renewable as solar or wind power. The other odd thing, of course, is that councils all over Britain are furiously chopping down trees as fast as they can, not for fuel but simply because trees are considered messy in that once a year they have a habit of distributing their leaves on the roadside. Worse still some trees, such as cherry and magnolia, insist on ignoring the rules about littering and allowing their blossom to fall where it may – invariably without obtaining permission from the requisite department.

Time
'All my possessions for a moment of time.' – *Elizabeth I*

Abuse
It is hard for anyone to remain resolute and dignified in a world where abuse is the commonest currency of expression.

Office 'Workers'
Office staff in central London (many of them civil servants) now work just 2.3 days a week. This is one of the lowest figures in the world. Could this possibly be linked to the fact that Britain has the worst productivity levels in the world?

The Bush Tavern Bill of Fare
A Bill of Fare for Christmas Day 1790, prepared for a Bristol coaching inn called the Bush Tavern, listed more than 100 dishes including turbot, eels, teal, coot, snipe, larks, widgeon, a veal's head, cuckoos, owls, golden plovers, swan, stares, sea pheasant, venison, reindeer tongues and a 47lb turtle. The pub also provided a roasting pig, 18 carp, six saddles of mutton, 116 pigeons and a vast variety of other game, meats and seafood. (Incidentally, the unfortunate turtle was a popular delicacy and was hunted almost to extinction. The gelatinous substances from the upper and lower shell, known as calipash and calipee, were regularly served at banquets. As the turtle grew rarer, cooks invented the mock turtle made from calves' heads. And so when Tenniel illustrated Alice's meeting with the Gryphon and the Mock Turtle he drew the turtle with the head of a calf. (I don't know why, but I thought you'd like to know all that.) Dickens visited the Bush Tavern in 1835 and used it as background in his novel *The Pickwick Papers*.

Booze
'I should have never switched from Scotch to Martinis.' – *Humphrey*

Long Live the Bouquinistes
I have always loved the bouquinistes along the banks of the Seine in Paris, and have spent many lovely hours browsing and buying. These green painted wooden boxes, which rest on the walls along the banks of the Seine, are full of books, prints and similar items. There are 240 boxes, and collectively they hold around 300,000 books. The boxes are a UNESCO World Heritage Site. Booksellers pay a small fee to the City of Paris and there is usually a waiting list of several years for a box. The bouquinistes have been in place for over 500 years, and it is said that the habit of selling books by the river began when a boat laden with books sank near Notre Dame in the early 16th century. The crew salvaged much of the cargo and sold the books on the river's banks. During World War II, the bouquinistes were much used in helping the French Resistance share messages. It has long been an ambition of mine to have control of a bouquinistes.

Skills
If you're good at art you become a painter. If you're good with cars you become a mechanic. If you're good at cheating and lying, and making promises you know you have no intention of keeping, then you become a politician. It was ever thus.

Circumstances
A man who was about to hang himself,
Finding a purse, then threw away his rope;
The owner, coming to reclaim his pelf,
The halter found, and used it. So is hope
Changed for Despair – one laid upon the shelf,
We take the other. Under Heaven's high cope
Fortune is God – all you endure and do

Depends on circumstances as much as you.
(Translated from the Greek by Percy Bysshe Shelley)

Justice

There is no justice without truth. But for years now the truth has been deliberately and systematically suppressed by the mainstream media (particularly the BBC) and by big internet companies such as Google (and their evil child YouTube) and Wikipedia. When the truth is hidden, and the truth-tellers are demonised and crushed, justice disappears.

People who were cruel to animals and people

There is a strong relationship between those who are cruel to animals and those who are cruel to humans – the sort of people who abuse animals are likely to abuse humans too.
1. Peter Kurten (aka the Dusseldorf Monster), practised bestiality on dogs and murdered more than 50 humans.
2. Luke Woodham, set fire to his own dog, stabbed his mother and killed two teenage girls.
3. David Berkowitz shot his neighbour's dog, poisoned his mother's parakeet and killed six people.
4. Patrick Sherrill stole local pets for his dog to attack and murdered 14 people.
5. Jack Bassenti buried puppies alive and raped and murdered people.
6. Edward Kemperer chopped up cats and killed his grandparents, his mother and seven other women.
7. Henry Lee Lucas killed animals and murdered his wife and mother.
8. Michael Cartier, threw a kitten through a closed window and pulled a rabbit's legs out of its sockets when he was four-years-old and grew up to become a murderer.
9. Randy Roth used an industrial sander on a frog, taped a cat to a car engine and killed two wives.

10. Jeffrey Dahmer killed many animals and 17 men.

African Queen
Almost the entire cast and crew making the film of C.S.Forrester's novel *African Queen* (including Katherine Hepburn) suffered from intestinal upsets caused by the drinking water with which they were supplied. The only two who did not suffer were the director (John Huston) and the male lead Humphrey Bogart. They drank whisky and avoided the water.

War
'History is littered with the wars which everybody knew would never happen.' – *Enoch Powell*

Floral clocks
The floral clock may be a small thing to mourn, but the demise of these horticultural timepieces has marked the end of civic pride. There was a time, not long ago, when any town worth its salt would have enough money to pay for a floral clock and a modest ornamental garden. Today, floral clocks are rarely seen.

Internet
The internet was supposed to connect us but it has driven us further and further apart. It has, ironically, disconnected us.

Mistreatment
For several years now everyone I know, or know of, who has been

treated in hospital has been misdiagnosed and, inevitably therefore, mistreated. That is no exaggeration. It is the truth.

Cement Mixer Man

A man in Yorkshire, England has travelled more than 200,000 miles looking for cement mixers to photograph. The enthusiast spent 15 years taking photographs of cement mixers and now has over 1,000 pictures in his collection. 'I used to be a train spotter,' he is reported to have said. 'But I found it boring.'

Sorry

'Pardon me, sir, I did not do it on purpose.' – *Marie Antoinette, after stepping on the executioner's foot when climbing up to the guillotine*

Spider

We had an insectivorous Venus fly trap. A spider spread a web over the plant to catch the flies attracted by the plant. The plant died. The spider lived.

Surgery

By the end of the 19th century, surgeons were able to operate on patients with a reasonable expectation that their patients would live. Surgeon even began doing elective surgery. And then they began doing operations for conditions that were inconvenient or troubling rather than life threatening. These developments were due to two things: an understanding of sepsis and the ability to put patients to sleep during operations (without getting them drunk or knocking them out). The understanding of sepsis meant surgeons could minimise the risk of infection by washing their hands, dressing in clean clothing and washing their surgical instruments in chlorinated-lime solution. The discovery of nitrous oxide, ether and chloroform led to anaesthesia.

Aspirin

In studies involving one million patients with 18 different cancers, about a quarter of the patients took 75mg of aspirin a day. Analysis showed a reduction of 21% in mortality among the patients who had taken the small dose of aspirin. Doctors are, however, still largely reluctant to recommend that people take prophylactic aspirin – despite its proven anti-inflammatory effect and its usefulness in protecting cancer patients and patients liable to heart attacks. A small daily dose of aspirin is extraordinarily cheap and seems to work well but there is virtually no profit in selling plain, common or garden soluble aspirin and so drug companies are uninterested. The medical establishment always does what it is told to do by the pharmaceutical industry.

Stephen Duck

Stephen Duck was an English poet who was enormously popular in the first half of the eighteenth century. He was at one point chaplain of Kew Palace. Queen Caroline was taken with him and gave him a small house in Richmond Park, together with an annuity. The first Lord Palmerston was also impressed by young Duck, who had dedicated a volume of his poetry to him, and in return wanted the inhabitants of Duck's birthplace to be rewarded. Palmerston therefore gave a piece of land (known as Duck's acre) with the instruction that the rent from the land should provide an annual feast for those adult males of Pewsey who were engaged in farming. The feast is held on June 1st every year at the Charlton Cat Inn near Pewsey in Wiltshire, England. The Duck Feast is the oldest dinner club in England. Only farmers or agricultural workers who are over 21 years of age and have lived in the parish for at least three years can attend, though since there are so few of them they usually invite some guests to join them. It is customary to invite the Vicar of St Peter's Church, Charlton and to ask his permission to ring the church bells before the feast begins. The Chief Duck wears a hat decorated with duck feathers and leads the toast to the poet.

Sadistic or stupid

After Antoinette had surgery for her breast cancer she was put into a chair because the ward had no beds. One of the nurses (a cold, sadistic creature if ever I've seen one, and the sort of woman who gave nursing a bad name in the days of Dickens) delivered a huge list of instructions so rapidly that I could hardly keep up. I thought they'd stopped making this particular model of nurse generations ago but it appears that the production line is still in full flow. She was talking to Antoinette but since Antoinette was semi-conscious this was rather a waste of time. Indeed, she was talking 'at' her rather than 'to' her. I scribbled down the things the nurse told Antoinette. Here are my notes: 'There may be bleeding. If there is, it could be a lot of bleeding and you need to come to the Accident and Emergency department straight away. You might develop a haematoma. If you do you need to come to the Accident and Emergency unit straight away. If you develop a fever you could have septicaemia. If so you must come to Accident and Emergency straight away. (The nurse did not mention the symptoms to look out for – fever, shivering, a fast pulse, shortness of breath, sweating.) You may have the worst pain you've ever had in your life.' (There was no indication about whether this terrifying consequence would be as a result of the bleeding, the haematoma, the septicaemia or some other unmentioned horror.) Mrs Gamp then gave Antoinette some drugs for her to take. There were some paracetamol tablets and some codeine tablets. (Hardly adequate for the worst pain of your life.) 'You must take them every two hours,' she told Antoinette. Actually, the box in which the pills came warned that they should not be taken more than every four hours. And the discharge sheet which was given to Antoinette advised that the drugs should be taken qds which is Latin shorthand and means four times a day. We were also given some dressings. 'You should not drive or operate machinery for two or three days. Don't do any carrying or housework for two weeks. Don't use the kettle for two weeks. Don't sign any legal documents for two days. Watch out for lymphedema. You must not get the dressing too wet. Don't raise your arms above your head. Do the exercises you've been given.' (One of the exercises involved raising the arms above the head) 'Don't let anyone take your blood pressure in your left arm. Ever. Don't let anyone take blood samples from your left arm. Ever. And remember that the risk of infection in that arm is greater than the other arm.' There may have been more instructions. That was everything I managed to scribble down. There were no words of reassurance or hope or comfort, there was no attempt at kindness or sympathy for a woman who had just had an operation for breast cancer – just warnings of potential death and disaster. It's a bit like getting on an aeroplane and listening to the stewardess warning you that the plane might crash and kill you. 'Welcome aboard this flight to Malaga. I must warn you that this aeroplane might crash at take-off or on landing or may fall out of the sky for no apparent reason. It may also be shot down by terrorists. Dolores and I will be bringing snacks around as soon as the seat belt sign has gone off. But the snacks may cause food poisoning.' And with those gloomy warnings from Mrs Gamp ringing in our ears we were sent on our way. (Actually, the words were only ringing in my ears. Antoinette hardly knew where she was.) In the bad old days no one was discharged from hospital without being seen by a doctor. These days there was no sign of a doctor anywhere. It did seem odd to me that the hospital didn't provide a printed leaflet containing all the advice that we were given. When it comes to forms they don't usually stint themselves. So, for example, Antoinette had been required to sign a form agreeing that the bag she had brought with her did not contain any money, credit cards or other valuables. At least that was what she was told it was about. Oh, and there was one other booklet: an expensively printed production (most official, taxpayer funded booklets are ridiculously expensively printed) which said that breast cancer patients should avoid stress.

Crowds

'Am I dying or is it my birthday?' – *Lady Nancy Astor, puzzled by the crowd around her bed*

Uniforms

In large hospitals these days there are charts stuck up in various places, usually showing that there are at least 20 basic uniforms for the staff. I wonder if anyone knows them all. There are coloured outfits and badges and different coloured ribbons. Everyone wears trousers and there are no white coats.

Pepys

Writing in his diary in 1665, Samuel Pepys wondered whether his good health was a result of his hare's-foot charm or the turpentine supplement he swallowed every morning. 'I am at a loss,' he wrote, 'to know whether it be my hare's foot which is my preservative for I never had a fit of colic since I wore it, or whether it be my taking of a pill of turpentine every morning. But this I know, with thanks to God Almighty, I am as well was ever I can wish to be.'

Forbidden or Allowed

'When the New World Order is here (and it getting very close), everything will be forbidden except that which is allowed. And everything will be allowed except that which is forbidden. But no one will know what is allowed and what is forbidden.' – *Jack King*

Mark Twain Speaking

Mark Twain once strode onto a stage and did not speak for ten minutes. Eventually, members of the audience began to laugh nervously. And so Twain, with his audience nicely primed and expectant, began to speak. This must have taken great courage. When I gave lectures about animal experimentation I used to stand on the stage for thirty seconds before starting to speak. I would ostentatiously look at my watch and at the end of thirty seconds I would tell the audience how many animals had died in laboratories in that period. Waiting thirty seconds seemed like an age and the audience would always get restless.

Dying
'Oh, I am not going to die, am I? He will not separate us, we have been so happy.' – *Charlotte Bronte*

Self-sacrifice
'I am just going outside and may be some time.' – *Captain Lawrence Oates, a member of Scott's expedition to the Antarctic in 1911-3, who was ill and was speaking just before he walked out into a blizzard to give his companions a better chance of surviving*

Christmas Bells
On Christmas Eve, in the parish of Dewsbury in Yorkshire, the tenor bell is tolled once for every year that has passed since the first Christmas. So, in the year 2000, the bell was rung 2,000 times. In the year 2100, the bell will be rung 2,100 times. The ringing is timed to end at exactly midnight. The bell ringing began in the late thirteenth or early fourteenth century and was started by Sir Thomas Soothill who gave the bell to the church. Those living within earshot of the church are probably immensely grateful for his generosity.

Caring

No one really seems to care anymore. I have a theory that this is because our society is criss-crossed with so many rules and regulations that the result is that no one has any sense of responsibility any more. You see this most evidently in those working for local or central government, but it's also apparent in the utility companies and it has spread into health care so doctors simply do what the rules say they should do (or what they think the rules say they should do or, possibly, what they believe the rules should say they should do.) Common sense has been crushed by rules and regulations. Not even doctors have the good sense or the humanity to realise that people are not machines and need to be treated according to their needs and not according to a rule on a website.

Shakespeare

In the 18th century, the search for papers relating to William Shakespeare became a stampede. In 1792, Samuel Ireland and his son William Henry arrived in Stratford upon Avon to search for old papers, manuscripts and ephemera. Just as they were about to leave and go home they met a man in a pub who told them to try a nearby farmer called Williams. They found Mr Williams. 'Do you know of any papers relating to William Shakespeare?' they asked. 'I wish you'd arrived a little sooner,' he replied. He told them that he had, two weeks earlier destroyed several basketfuls of letters and papers, some with Shakespeare's name upon them. 'I told you not to burn the papers,' said Mrs Williams. But the disappointed Ireland didn't give up. In 1794, Ireland claimed to have found the manuscript of King Lear, a love letter from a young Shakespeare to his beloved Anna Hatherrewaye (together with a lock of Shakespeare's hair), correspondence with the Earl of Southampton, letters to Shakespeare from Queen Elizabeth, and two previously unknown and unpublished plays 'Henry II' and 'Vortigern and Rowena'. London's literary men went wild with delight. Famous people queued to see the documents which were, in due course, taken along to St James's Palace and Carlton House to be viewed by royalty. Sadly, the bubble was burst by spoilsport know-it-all scholars. Mr Ireland, it seemed, had created everything himself. He used old paper cut out of ancient books, together with some ancient vellum, and physically the material he had 'discovered' was convincing. Sadly, however, he didn't manage to imitate 16th century style and spelling and his hoax ended in exposure and shame. It was by no means the first literary hoax, and would certainly not be the last, but Mr Ireland has to be given full marks for ambition.

Too Bright
'Since cricket became brighter, a man of taste can only go to an empty ground and regret the past. Or else watch a second-class county match and regret the future.' – *C.P.Snow*

Loopholes
When he was asked why he was reading the Bible, W.C.Fields, who was dying, replied: 'I am looking for loopholes'.

Bad Grace
Millennials and snowflakes seem to do less and less work with an increasingly bad grace.

Backbone
It is generally and widely believed that the backbone is the sine qua non of the human skeleton, and that without it the rest of the structure will collapse in an untidy heap. This is now known to be nonsense. No politician of this century has, or has had, even the rudimentary vestiges of a backbone.

Duty
'You know what to do, take care of my dear Lady Hamilton, Hardy, take care of poor Lady Hamilton. Kiss me, Hardy.' – *Admiral Horatio Nelson, on HMS Victory, dying at the Battle of Trafalgar in 1805. Nelson had insisted on standing on deck in his full uniform, with all medals visible, cheering his men but giving the enemy's sharpshooters an easy target.*

Collector
Some people collect beer mats, ashtrays or train numbers; others collect postage stamps or hotel towels. A television presenter whom I knew admitted that he collected washbasin plugs (together with their chains) which he tore from sinks in studios and hotels. He had a collection of over 450 plugs and chains, mostly black and pretty much identical. He told me he kept them in a large box in his garage. To each one was attached a small label describing the plug's origin. 'They're much easier to steal than towels or bathrobes,' he said, 'because they are smaller and no one thinks anyone would want to steal one.' He told me that he did not steal bath plugs. 'Why would I steal bath plugs?' he asked, apparently disturbed by the thought. 'What are you going to do with them all?' I asked him. He was quite unable to answer the question, which was something he had clearly never considered.

Change
'We grow to dislike change very much when we get old. This is because the ultimate and unavoidable change is death and the older you get the more it becomes apparent that there is no escape route.' – *Flavio Cipollini*

Doctors
Referring to doctors by their Christian names (as in 'Dr John' or 'Dr Mary') manages to combine some superficial and faux friendliness, and a sense of equality, while at the same time preserving the doctor's acquired sense of professional dignity and aloofness.

Odd
I have always thought it odd that the same dose of a prescribed drug is given to all patients – whatever their size. So a woman who is seven stones in weight will be given exactly the same dose as a man or woman who weighs three times as much. This is, of course, woefully unscientific.

Books
I buy huge numbers of books (well over a thousand a year) and I reckon that up to one in five non-fiction books that I buy are so heavily marked (with ink markings, highlighting and comments scribbled in the margin) that they are useless and should have been dumped rather than sold. No bookshop (not even a junk shop) would ever try to sell such heavily marked books to live, walking, talking, actually being there customers but greedy and uncaring online sellers think they can get away with it because their buyers can't see what they are getting. I sometimes write notes in my own books but once I've done so I would never dream of trying to sell them, or of giving them away to a charity shop. This habit of selling heavily marked books is even more annoying than the habit of putting stickers on books which can't be removed without damaging the cover or the jacket.

Everyone will be above average
A large survey showed that 94% of people in any group now rate

themselves above average at doing whatever they do (whether it be driving a motor car, investing or making love). What's the betting that the figure will be closer to 100% in five years' time? Is it likely that members of the Z generation will ever regard themselves as being average, or below average, at anything?

Athletes

'There is an enthusiasm these days for banning athletes whose blood contains too much of whichever naturally occurring hormone is considered helpful in whatever their sport might be. This seems desperately unfair to those individuals whose bodies naturally contain too much of whichever substance is considered to bestow an advantage on its user. Athletes have, I gather, been told that because they have too much of this or that then, before they can compete, they must have some of this or that removed – even though the this or that occurs naturally in their bodies.

I'm puzzled because if Miss X is to be banned from her chosen sport because her body is richer in, say, natural testosterone than those of other athletes, shouldn't there be bans preventing other well-endowed individuals from competing in sports?

Individuals brought up in areas which are a long way above sea level (Kenya or Mexico City) have huge advantages over individuals brought up at sea level when they compete in long distance events since their blood can carry far more oxygen. Indians living in the Andes have three more pints of blood in their bodies than people who live at sea-level. In some events it would be virtually impossible for someone born in New York, Paris or London to beat a native of the Andes. Tall people have a huge advantage over short people when playing basketball. And large, heavily built individuals are more likely to be successful at events like putting the shot and throwing the hammer. So, maybe each event should rule out all contestants who are likely to have an advantage over other contestants. Basketball teams should only include players who are under 5 feet 8 inches tall, for example, and only people who are under 5 feet 6 inches tall and weigh less than 9 stones should be allowed to throw the hammer.' – *Daniel J Beddowes*

Cary Grant
'Grant wouldn't do any of the numerous movies proposed to him over the years after 1965. It just wasn't to be because Cary did not want his aged appearance to alter the essential screen image he had projected since 1932. I once complained, in the late seventies or early eighties, that here we'd known each other all these years and my two daughters had never even met him and he said: 'Well, you don't want to frighten the poor dears, do you? I mean they think they're going to meet Cary Grant and in comes this old man in a wheelchair.' – *Peter Bogdanovitch*

Arty Farty
'To begin with, some modern art meant something. Look back to the 19th century and the start of the 20th century and we see a world ablaze with ideas and talent.

Artists who had difficulty expressing themselves in traditional ways explored many new styles. Inspired by the genius of Turner, painters such as Van Gogh, Monet, Manet, Picasso, Utrillo, Braque, Matisse and Chagall delighted millions.

Gradually, however, artists became lazy, self-obsessed and trivial. And most people lost interest; regarding modern art as irrelevant, foolish and unenlightened.

The big unasked (and therefore unanswered) question is 'Does modern art reflect our culture or is our culture merely a manifestation of modern art?' In other words, has our hollow, cruel, selfish, ugly culture led to hollow, cruel, selfish, ugly art? Or is it the other way around?

Whatever the answer might be there is no doubt that there must be a connection.

The glories of the Renaissance and the spiritual values of the Age of Reason were left behind a long time ago. The sort of paintings which we used to regard as 'Art' (and which, I suspect, most people still think of as Art) aren't just pictorial representations but reflect human values, hopes, fears and expectations. Paintings aren't just pretty pictures to cover up damp patches on damp walls in damp houses, but they contain messages to be shared between the mind of the artist and the eye of the beholder. Whatever the style might have been, society and art influenced one another.

Today, modern art is mainly just silly and artists are self-indulgent, unoriginal and out of touch. It is not uncommon for expensive modern art to be hung upside down without anyone noticing. When even curators don't have the foggiest which way up to hang something then I would question whether it can be described as art at all. And I rather lost all respect for modern art when a banana which had been duct-taped to a wall was offered for sale at $110,000. When a visitor picked the banana off the wall and ate it, the 'artist' went to a local greengrocer, purchased another banana and replaced his artwork. The Emperor's new clothes are widely praised by critics and dealers who are too nervous to expose what they are seeing for what it is.

In art, literature and all forms of entertainment the aim now is to shock. Young artists seem to think that their only way of making their mark is to do something startling rather than clever, and crude rather than creative. The artist who studies and learns and produces beautiful landscapes, still life paintings or skilful portraits will be ignored while the 'artist' who ignores the basic requirements of art but specialises in learning about marketing and then combines circus skills with contacts among dealers and gallery owners will go far.

And I read this in a catalogue: 'X's autoethnographic work is concerned with formalising 'in between' spaces drawing on feelings associated with loss and abandonment from his childhood experiences. He has cultivated a schism in his art practice that manifests in crossing the boundary of sculpture and drawing, objects or materials being removed from one place and placed in another and subject matter of physical spaces that are between states. Through allusions his work triggers metaphors and personal associations which allow the viewer to contemplate ambivalence.'

The accompanying artwork was entitled 'Pencil leads with paper pulp' and consisted of pencil leads arranged in the form of a nest, lined with the paper pulp'. It was priced at £2,750.

An extraordinary piece of so-called art by Cy Twombly (it's official name is 'Untitled' but it also seems to be titled 'Bacchus 1st

Version 11') went for $19.96 million in 2023. The 'art' was catalogued by Christies New York with these words 'It might track the upward flight-path of spirit in rapture, or a cataclysm of debauched violence'. The viewer presumably takes their pick. The painting consists of splodges of paint, brushed onto a canvas and having run in lines to the bottom.

Twombly also produced a piece of 'art' consisting of nothing more than scribbles made with paint, coloured pencil and wax crayon. In an attempt to justify the work as 'art' one critic wrote: 'Frequently likened to a child's doodles, this scribbled image, which remained stubbornly at variance with US art after World War II, appears easy enough for a young child to have done. Yet the spare, messy and often indistinct scribbles were not created through a lack of skill or understanding of depth. They are an exploration of human existence, reflecting on and connecting with classical art and literature.'

An 'artist' called Barnett Newman produced some unusual modern art. One of his 'paintings' consists of a strip of masking tape stuck vertically down the centre of a painted canvas with another colour painted over it.

'Any child could do that,' wrote a critic with unusual and disarming honesty, 'but none would do so in order to make statements about the modern world needing new and powerful kinds of art – art that expresses and invokes intuition and aspirations.'

Another so-called piece of art consisted of a canvas with a knife slash down the middle. 'No child could have done that,' remarked one critic. 'Who would allow a child to handle a knife that sharp?'

The lunacy hasn't just infected individual artists. It has become institutionalised and corporate. Museums used to be buildings dedicated to the display of fine paintings, sculpture and other artefacts. Today there is a Disgusting Food Museum in Malmo, Sweden; a Museum of Ice Cream in San Francisco; a Museum of Broken Relationships in Zagreb, Croatia and a Museum of Failure in Helsingborg, Sweden.

Curiously, although most people are well aware that the Emperor is parading around quite naked, governments continue to subsidise crappy art (usually described as 'culture') so that, although no one is prepared to pay for it, it can be made available free of charge to, well, anyone who is interested in it – probably because it is raining and the gallery is the nearest place to go.

Huge amounts of taxpayers' money are paid to these self-styled artists (and their colleagues producing so-called poetry, plays and sculpture) despite the fact that no one wants their work.' – *Jack King*

Universal Ignorance
'Nobody knows anything.' – *William Goldman*

Health Care
The US and the UK have the most expensive health care in the world. They also have the worst health care in the world.

Fight
The real fight isn't between the left and the right. The real fight is between the billionaires, the bankers and the bloated plutocrats and the rest of us.

Loan Car
Our truck was in the garage and for boring and complicated reasons the repair was going to take three weeks. (In brief, the cheapskate manufacturer in Japan decided to save themselves three-pence by sending a relatively small replacement part by ship rather than by aeroplane. No names and no pack drill but I shan't ever buy anything made by Mitsubishi again.) The garage lent us a car. We drove into a nearby town to do some shopping. When we'd finished we headed back to the car park.

'Can you remember where we parked the car?' I asked as we struggled along with full shopping bags.

Antoinette thought for a moment. 'No, not really,' she said.

'No, nor me,' I confessed. We entered the car park. 'And I can't remember the car number.'

'I never thought to look,' said Antoinette. 'What make is it?'

'I have no idea. And there's no maker's name on the key.'

'We could walk around while you press the unlocking button on the key-ring,' said Antoinette.

'The button doesn't work,' I said. 'Can you remember anything about the car which would help identify it?'

Antoinette thought for a moment. 'It's small and a sort of dirty grey.'

In a car park containing 600 cars do you have any idea how many of them match that description?

We wandered round, trying hard not to look like car thieves (and doubtless looking just like very ineffectual car thieves) as I tried the car key in umpteen door locks – hoping it was not true that car manufacturers sometimes used the same key to fit several cars.

It took us 19 minutes to find a car that the car key fitted.

And even when we handed the car back to the garage a few days later I was still not entirely sure it was the right little, grey car.

Lingerie

Underwear is designed to keep you warm and decent. Lingerie, on the other hand, is designed to be an inspiration to both the wearer and the viewer. The effectiveness of skilfully designed lingerie is proven by the fact that back in the 17th century, the English Parliament ruled that a woman who trapped a man into marriage with the aid of a bosom boosted by fancy folderols would be tried for witchcraft and the marriage annulled.

Rights

If you live in the UK, the Government now has the right to take your organs out of body without your permission and while you are still alive. (There is no point in removing organs from a dead body.). And the Government also has the right to share your confidential medical information with the world's drug companies. Those are both the default position. You can opt out if you wish though whether or not your decisions will be obeyed is moot.

Fingerprints

In the 19th century, first time offenders in Britain were given shorter prison sentences than recidivists. But the authorities had a problem: how could they identify new offenders? It was too easy for accomplished criminals to give a false name and hope not to be recognised. And so fingerprints were introduced. Other countries (including France, Japan and India) had used them so the idea wasn't new.

Superman

The CV of a man called Aleksey Garber was given some coverage in the *New Yorker* magazine. Mr Gerber, a student, submitted his CV to various investment banks. He claimed he had taught tennis to Jerry Seinfeld and Harrison Ford and won two games in a match against Pete Sampras. He said he had mastered the art of bone setting and was a specialist in Chinese orthopaedic massage. He claimed he had taken part in a skiing competition in Switzerland, been on the CIA firing range and taken part in a martial arts competition in secret tunnels under Woodstock. His CV said he had forged passports for the Russian mafia and that he charged two hundred dollars an hour as a model. He said he had written a book entitled *Women's Silent Tears: A Unique Gendered Perspective on the Holocaust*, served as an advisor at an investment firm, founded a charity for troubled children, taken up ballroom dancing (with the international rumba a speciality) and could bench press nearly 500 pounds. He said he could serve a tennis ball at 140 miles per hour and split a stack of bricks with his bare hand. He claimed to be one of four people licensed to handle nuclear waste in the state of Connecticut and said that he had to register his hands as lethal weapons at airports, and had killed two dozen men in Tibetan gladiatorial contests. I do not know if Mr Garber was offered employment.

Hippocratic Oath

When I qualified as a doctor I was invited to take the Hippocratic Oath. It was optional. Some young doctors said they would. Many said they wouldn't. Today, the Hippocratic Oath is considered out of date. The General Medical Council in the UK (the body with the job of licensing doctors) thinks the Oath is now irrelevant and, indeed, supports the idea of doctors breaking the tradition of consulting room confidentiality.

Here, so that you can make up your own mind, are the principle and relevant sections of the Hippocratic Oath:

'I swear that I will carry out, according to my ability and judgement, this oath.

I will use those dietary regimens which will benefit my patients according to my greatest ability and judgement, and I will do no harm or injustice to them. Neither will I administer a poison to anybody when asked to do so, nor will I suggest such a course. But I will keep pure and holy both my life and my art. I will not use the knife, not even, verity on sufferers from stone, but I will give place to such as are craftsmen therein.

Into whatsoever houses I enter, I will enter to help the sick, and I will abstain from all intentional wrong doing and harm, especially from abusing the bodies of man or woman, bond or free. And whatsoever I shall see or hear in the course of my profession I will never divulge, holding such things to be holy secrets.

Now if I carry out this oath and break it not, may I gain for ever reputation among all men for my life and for my art; but if I break it and forswear myself, may the opposite befall me.

(Note: you will see that the Hippocratic Oath forbids euthanasia/doctor assisted suicide.)

Paper Doctors

In my book *Paper Doctors* (first published in 1977 but now

republished and available to discerning readers) I called for an end to medical research, arguing that we already had masses of useful knowledge which we never use and that the world would be a much better, healthier place if we looked for ways to take advantage of the things we have learned. I still believe that was right. (As an aside, *Paper Doctors* has been rare and unavailable for years. When I decided to reprint it, I found I hadn't got a copy and had to buy one for £200 from a rare book shop in the USA.)

Fact Checkers

The official definition of a 'fact-checker' is: 'a corrupt, uneducated individual; someone who is easily corrupted; someone who denies the truth and promotes lies in return for generous payments and advancement'. – *Zina Cohen*

Anniversary

I've always thought it important to have a mental library of special days – hours or minutes or even moments when things seemed to go just right.

You cannot deliberately create special or memorable days. They usually just happen. Serendipity rules! But with a little thoughtful planning it is possible to manage the circumstances so that a day has a greater chance of being special and I like to think that our plans for our wedding anniversary in 2019 played a small part in making it one of those days we will both remember forever. But the biggest influence, of course, was God.

We drove to Bicton Park in Devon and for a start, God was kind to us. He gave us one of those gloriously sunny, crisp winter days which are perfect for walking in the countryside.

Since it was a trifle chilly to eat outside (even for us) we decided to have a picnic in the car. I asked for marmalade sandwiches and a small flask of Lapsang Souchong tea. Antoinette made the sandwiches and put them in a small brown paper bag. I always refer to Lapsang Souchong as bonfire tea because the smell reminds me of bonfires. No drink works better in a hot flask. (Laphroaig would have worked even better but I was driving.)

Then we went to St Mary's church which was, as it usually seems to be, quite deserted. It was colder inside the church than it was outside, but that didn't matter. We read the Prayer of Thanksgiving which I had written and I gave Antoinette an eternity ring, as a commemorative symbol of our first 20 years together. I also gave her a haiku which I had written:

Music, toys and cards
Give smiles and joy; no question
Love's the gift forever

We then left, before we froze, and put £10 each into the donations box by the door as a thank you for the loan of the church. Our next important anniversary will be our 25th. I pray God is kind enough to take us there and give us a similarly joyful day. And then we set off to wander around the park.

The first thing we saw was a pair of robins. As Antoinette pointed out, you don't usually see two robins together in December. These two, presumably a pair, were the best of chums. And then, a minute later, we spotted two Red Admiral butterflies sunning themselves on the bark of a huge oak tree. You don't usually see butterflies out and about in December. Moreover, these didn't have that battered look that seems common among winter butterflies. These looked fresh and full of colour.

And then we walked for a while. And then we went home.

In the evening I lit a roaring log fire and we watched John Ford's 'The Quiet Man' starring John Wayne and Maureen O'Hara – surely one of the most romantic films ever made. Tomorrow we will watch 'The Thin Man', with William Powell and Myrna Loy. Yesterday evening we watched 'African Queen' with Humphrey Bogart and Katherine Hepburn. And as back-up we have 'The Thirty Nine Steps' with Robert Donat and Madeleine Carroll and 'Mr Blandings Builds his Dream House' with Cary Grant and Myrna Loy.

What a day. What a memory. In my experience the very best days are so often simple and uncomplicated.

And below is the prayer I wrote for the occasion of our 20th wedding anniversary on our 20th Anniversary on 3rd December 2019. (Just months earlier Antoinette had been diagnosed with breast cancer and been through an arduous treatment programme.)

Dear Lord,

As You know, we have been together as man and wife for 20 years today. Finding each other, and our true love for each other, is the most wonderful thing that has happened to us. On this special day we would like to renew the vows we took two decades ago. We thank You for bringing us together and turning two lives into one and we promise, in Your presence, to love, honour and respect each other through joy and sadness, through good and through bad, through hope and through despair; all ways and always, and for eternity. We ask You to acknowledge and bless the bond that exists between us and which has given us the strength to deal with life's vicissitudes. We thank You for bringing us together and making our lives whole and we ask You to recognise our eternal love for each other. Please bless our marriage with peace and happiness and strengthen our bodies, minds and spirits at what is, as You know, the most difficult time of our lives. Thanks to Your wisdom, oh Lord, we are as one person. Please Lord give us the strength to live our life together with passion, courage and wisdom. Bless our marriage and our togetherness, dear Lord. We thank You for the past 20 years of togetherness and unity and we beseech You, oh Lord, to give us strength of body, mind and spirit for the years ahead. In the name of Jesus Christ.

Amen.

Doctors and Respect

Doctors have only themselves to blame if they find that they are treated with less respect than their professional predecessors. You cannot work the sort of hours favoured by part time book-keepers and expect to be loved. And doctors who go on strike for more money can expect to be treated with the level of respect enjoyed by stevedores and train drivers.

Fame

Fame and a sense of self-importance can have a funny effect on people.

When I was young I used to make a great many television programmes. (I was on television so often that I had to become a member of Equity.) I discovered that the best thing about making a TV series is that you get your hair cut regularly for the sake of continuity. This means there is no need to visit a barber.

I remember making a series with a professional singer who was good fun and quite charming.

And then they had a hit record.

And how they changed.

I remember sitting next to them in the make-up department one day when one of the hairdressers came over and very politely asked them if they would do an interview with her niece, a member of the BBC's radio station news team, which worked in the same building.

'It'll mean a lot to her,' she said. 'She's very young and only started this job ten days ago.'

'No,' said the singer, who was sitting doing nothing. 'I'm too busy.' They didn't even apologise or soften the rejection. It was a very bald 'No'.

'Just five minutes, whenever and wherever it's convenient,' said the hairdresser. 'I said I'd ask for her. It would be a great start for her.'

'I said No,' snapped the singer.

The hairdresser, blushing with embarrassment, backed away as a courtier might back away from a bad tempered Queen.

The singer turned to me and rolled their eyes.

Four Leaf Clovers

George Kaminski, a long-term prisoner in Pennsylvania prisons, has collected 72,927 four leaf clovers in the grounds of the various prisons where he has been a guest. I hope they bring him luck.

The Centre of the Universe

When I was a young author, I used to travel around the country for three weeks at a time doing interviews on local television and local radio and for local newspapers. It was a surreal experience. Everywhere I went people were talking about my book – and about little else. Every news programme carried promotions for my book. Every newspaper journalist I met was desperate to know more about my book. I can understand how people who are forever in the public eye become convinced that the world revolves around them, and everything they do. I did not find it a particularly enjoyable experience. Sometimes, while on tour, I became disorientated. I remember once finding myself on a road to East Anglia and having to ring my publishers to find out why on earth I was going there.

Self-Cleaning

While visiting a hospital I sat at a table marked self-cleaning and wondered what this meant. I know that there are cars which can drive themselves but I did not realise that they had invented tables which cleaned themselves. I put my paper cup down on the table rather nervously, and wondered when the cleaning would start and what would happen. But nothing did happen and after a while I saw an obese man clearing away the debris of a carbohydrate heavy meal. When he had put his plates and cup and cutlery into various bins I watched him wipe the table with a paper tissue. I felt rather silly.

Self-Storage

The growth of self-storage depots is almost entirely a consequence of the enthusiasm of people for buying more stuff than they have room to store at home. I am assured that the people who rent these self-storage lockers (some of which are as big as decent sized rooms) frequently visit once a week so that they can look at their stuff, chat with their chairs, and fondle their books and old records in much the same sort of way that they might visit an elderly relative. And, although it is almost certainly against the rules, it seems that some people spend the night in their self-storage lockers, locking themselves in with their bric-a-brac, and the flotsam and jetsam they cannot bring themselves to abandon.

Free Macaroni Cheese for Life

Carlos Yulo, a gymnast from the Philippines who won two gold medals at the 2024 Olympics held in Paris, was given £218,000 and a medal from his government. He was also given a three bedroom property worth £436,000, headlights for his car and a lifetime supply of macaroni cheese. I have two unanswered questions. How did he come to have a car without headlights? And how long will it be before he grows to hate macaroni cheese?

Keith Floyd

Antoinette and I gave up watching television some years ago. These days we use our TV set solely for watching videos. We recently dug out a box set of programmes made by Keith Floyd, generally agreed to have been the greatest television cook of all time. Floyd was a natural showman, eccentric and probably difficult to work with, but a genius in front of a TV camera. In the end, Floyd's habit of drinking wine (and smoking) while presenting his programmes probably did for him. Towards the end of his life he was regarded as just too politically incorrect and, sadly, he was ignored and largely forgotten. I'm not usually interested in watching television cooks but Floyd was different: he was, without a doubt, the best television performer who has ever existed. There will never be anyone to match him.

The Editor

A newspaper editor and I were having lunch at the Savoy Hotel in London.

He ordered steak. When it arrived he poked it with his knife and then shouted at the waiter. 'Take this back,' he ordered. He gave instructions, explaining what was wrong with the steak and how it should be cooked. The red-faced waiter backed away, with the editor's plate in his hand.

'There was nothing wrong with it,' said the editor to me with a smirk. 'But you have to keep these people in their place.'

I promise you this story is true.

Christmas

'It is not difficult to imagine a world in which Christmas (as a part of the Christian faith) will be outlawed as an irrelevance which is considered offensive to those who worry (usually unnecessarily) about the sensibilities of non-Christians. It is not difficult to imagine such a world. But I wouldn't want to live in it.' – *J.Hutton*

Antiques

Antique shops may buy junk and bric a brac but they only ever sell antiques.

Life

'I had a good life. I think we are all scared of the day when we die, but life is about death as well. You have to learn to accept it for what it is. Hopefully, at the end people will say, 'Yeah, he was a good man', but everyone will not say that. I hope you will remember me as the positive guy trying to do everything he could do. Don't be sorry, smile. Thank you for everything, coaches, players, the crowds, it's been fantastic. Take care of yourself, and take care of your life. And live it. Bye.' – *Sven-Goran Eriksson (when he was dying)*

Retired

'The snag with retirement is that you don't really notice when you're on holiday.' – *M.Orton*

Flowers

There always used to be flower shops next to hospitals. If there wasn't a florist there would be a stall selling flowers. These days the shops next to hospitals are usually undertakers. Instead of being full of colourful flowers, their windows are decorated with urns and wreaths. The florists have gone because hospitals don't like flowers. Nurses refuse to have anything to do with flowers because they think that putting flowers into vases is beneath them. And they worry that flowers will need fresh water and will drop their petals as they die. I know this because I have asked many nurses why they don't like having flowers on the wards. I'm afraid that these nurses know nothing of medical history and little about human beings because every civilisation except ours has recognised the healing powers of flowers. And for thousands of years hospital wards were brightened with vases of flowers.

Flood alert 1

'There are still naïve people around who don't realise that the floods which have caused so much distress in recent years were planned, designed and created. Councils allowed building companies to erect houses on flood plains. They then let the rivers silt up so that when it rained the surrounding areas were flooded. Everyone then expressed surprise.' – *Philippa Rowe*

Flood alert 2

'The enthusiasm for sending out scary weather alerts reached a new peak for me when I received a terrifying email from our local council (complete with red banner headline) to tell me that there was absolutely no flood alert in our area. Since our village is on the top of a hill and at least 400 feet above the nearest natural water source this was a considerable comfort.' – *Philippa Rowe*

Hand Dryers

The loos in our nearest hospital are equipped with hand dryers which blow hot air upwards. This seems an excellent way to fire bugs into the faces of those using the dryers. Maybe the hospital is trying to boost its business.

Joy

On several glorious occasions I watched professional cricketers Barry Richards and Gordon Greenidge open the batting for Hampshire County Cricket Club in the English County Championship. There is now no point in my watching more cricket; nothing can ever match their brutal but controlled and delicious glory.

Investing

'Buy on the cannons, sell on the trumpets.' This is traditional advice given to investors and said to have originated with the Rothschild family. The idea is that buying shares when war starts tends to be far more profitable than buying them when peace is declared.

Raft

Like many other movie stars George Raft turned down leading parts in a number of very successful films. For example, he turned down High Sierra and The Maltese Falcon and in both cases was replaced by Humphrey Bogart. Towards the end of his life, Raft lived on $800 a month (social security and pension) and when he died all his belongings were offered for sale for $800.

The Medicine Men
The medical establishment sold itself to the drug industry years ago. In 1975, in my first book *The Medicine Men*, I pointed out that a profession that takes instructions from an industry can hardly call itself a profession. Today, doctors are just part of the marketing arm of the drugs industry. And whatever the drug industry decides about any aspect of medicine is accepted by the medical establishment as normal and essential.

Disposable heroes
Have you noticed that our heroes today are mostly superficial, trivial, interchangeable and quite disposable? Other generations had proper heroes – exceptional men and women whose exploits were inspirational. Today's so-called 'heroes' are builders, phone salesmen, modestly talented professional sports persons and pop singers who have succeeded in making themselves rich and famous but cannot properly be described as in any way heroic.

Inflation
It is not widely known but governments use a short list of items to decide on their country's official rate of inflation. The lists vary from country to country. Luxuries such as rent, heating, fuel and food are usually excluded from the list. If the cost of the selected items in the 'basket' goes up, then inflation goes up. And vice versa.

The latest list of items used to determine the inflation rate in England and Wales is reported to be as follows:
Stained glass windows
Quill pens
Tam o'shanter bonnets
Spats

Stagecoach tickets
Whalebone corsets
The 1966 Highway Code
Goose liver
Buggy whips
Hymn books
Miners' helmets
Silk top hats

Sports

Most sports stars have no knowledge or experience outside their chosen professions. They are, for all practical purposes, stuck between the ages of 12 and 15. If they are good enough to succeed at their sport this won't matter until they retire. But if they are not in the top 100 worldwide in their sport then their lives are destined to become barren deserts of disappointment.

Words of comfort

'Am I going to die from this cancer?' asked Antoinette, before going to the operating theatre.

'Well, there is a risk that you might,' replied the surgeon, a woman, who knew that Antoinette had suffered from anxiety and depression for a decade as a result of her sub-acute combined degeneration of the cord. When you warn people they might die then they tend to die. That's how voodoo works. The doctor is the most powerful of placebos.

It seemed to me (and still seems to me) to be an unforgivably wicked and blood curdlingly moronic thing to say.

If the surgeon believed that to be true and didn't want to lie (even to give a patient comfort) she could have said something anodyne such as: 'You're going to be fine'.

But oh no.

'There's a risk that you might (die).'

It seared into Antoinette's heart.

It would sear into anyone's heart.

Too many people just don't know how to care anymore.

And large hospitals, like all large organisations, exist to protect and secure themselves and so, inevitably, that is how the staff think and behave. Almost everything they do is done to keep the system happy and, most important of all, to protect their organisation from legal action.

Hospital staff members are instructed by the organisations lawyers that they must give patients a raft of warnings. And the result is health care which provides less in the way of kindness and compassion than the average Post Office. There has always been an element of defensiveness in the way medicine is practised. But the defensiveness now seems to take priority over everything else.

It is said that everyone in the finance industry is in sales – they all want to flog you something. In medicine the priority is avoiding litigation – and that takes precedence over everything else. The law now requires doctors and nurses to tell patients all the risks associated with every procedure (except vaccinations, of course). And the patient must sign forms absolving the medical staff from all responsibility. Medicine today is controlled not by doctors but by lawyers, economists and bureaucrats.

Duelling

Two surgeons I knew had a huge row and decided to settle their differences with a duel. Since neither they nor anyone they knew had any swords or pistols they agreed to duel with syringes. They chose 20 ml syringes as their weapons of choice and, after some practice, decided that they should stand 12 feet apart. The syringes were filled with a weak solution of Valium and the two protagonists wore motorcycle masks with visors to protect their faces. After three attempts they gave up. They and their seconds had by then become hysterical with laughter and they repaired to the hospital canteen for coffee and Danish pastries, with the cause of their duel forgotten. A lifetime of resentment had been avoided. Maybe duelling should be reintroduced.

Future
'The good thing about the future is that it comes one day at a time.'
– *Abraham Lincoln*

Trickery
'A scientist once told me that there was as much petty dishonesty and mean trickery (in science) as in high finance.' – *C.P.Snow*

Victoria
'The Queen is most anxious to enlist everyone who can speak or write to join in checking this mad, wicked folly of Women's Rights.'
– *Queen Victoria*

Cancer Frequency
In 'developed' countries around the world, it has for decades been said that one in three people will develop cancer. Since the rollout of the toxic covid-19 vaccine, it is generally agreed that one in two people will develop cancer. You can draw your own conclusion.

Sergeant
A sergeant who was retiring after distinguished war service (he had been in the army from 1939 to 1945) had a retirement medical. The doctor who conducted the examination spotted that the soldier had a glass eye. It transpired that the sergeant had lost his left eye in an accident in 1938, when he was just 18, but had remained determined to join the army. He tricked the doctors with a simple ploy. When he was asked to cover his right eye to read the chart he covered his left

eye (the one that didn't work) and read the chart. When he was asked to cover his left eye he covered his left eye and read the chart. Eventually, he simply 'borrowed' the eye chart that was used and memorised it.

Time

Everyone knows that you can buy money with your time. But only the wisest realise that you can also buy time with your money. Time is the most important, most fundamental currency in the world; the only currency that really matters.

PGW

It is a curious thing, but humans tend to punish those who dare to struggle in adversity and who show signs of possessing an indomitable spirit – particularly if it is allied to a sense of the absurd as well as a sense of humour.

During World War II, the much-loved English author P.G.Wodehouse was imprisoned by the Nazis for being in the wrong place at the wrong time (he was 59-years-old and living at his home in Le Touquet in Northern France when the Germans arrested him for being there). Placed in an internment camp, Wodehouse kept his fellow inmates cheered by telling them endless stories about his capture.

When the Germans finally realised that they had, by accident, 'captured' one of the most famous writers in the world, they persuaded him to broadcast a series of talks for Allied consumption. Innocently, naively, Wodehouse agreed, thinking that he could bring a little comfort and hope to the fretting relatives of those in the camps. His talks were typically whimsical. 'Young men starting out in life have often asked me, 'How can I become an internee?' Well, there are several methods. My own was to buy a villa in Le Touquet on the coast of France and stay there till the Germans came along.'

He compared the internment camp where he was imprisoned to a boys' boarding school.

But Wodehouse's refusal to be bowed by his capture did not go down well with some in England. Prodded into indignation by politicians, who had agendas of their own, a mean, snarky journalist called William Connor, hiding behind the pseudonym 'Cassandra', attacked Wodehouse in the *Daily Mirror* and on the BBC. In his libellous attacks, and with no evidence for his claims, Connor accused Wodehouse of being a traitor.

For Wodehouse, the consequences were dire. He fled to America and never returned to England. Professionally and personally he suffered enormously and could not understand what all the fuss was about. He had been pilloried for being honest and for trying to do a little good.

After the war, Wodehouse was slowly rehabilitated. His book sales recovered and, as the truth became known, public opinion moved in his favour and against Connor whose attacks were regarded as unjustified and cruel.

The shameless and unpleasant Connor, who was by then describing himself as a friend of Wodehouse (the man he'd tried so hard to destroy), then had the audacity to beg the author to go easy on him when talking on American television and radio about the whole affair.

And Wodehouse, being a very old-fashioned English gentleman, without a bad thought in his body (except, perhaps, about taxmen – he once remarked that the only way to deal with them was with an axe) was as gentle and forgiving as Connor no doubt knew he would be. He even persuaded Evelyn Waugh not to attack Connor.

Chemicals

'They found more dangerous chemicals in Coca-Cola's Dasant mineral water than they did in the whole of Iraq.' – *Robin Cook (a former British Foreign Secretary who resigned from his position as Leader of the House of Commons in protest against the invasion of Iraq. Cook later died in what are, by some, considered strange circumstances.)*

Mass of men

'The mass of men serve the state not as men but as machines, with their bodies. They are the standing army and the jailers and the constables. In most cases there is no free exercise whatsoever of the judgement or of the moral sense; but they put themselves on a level with wood and earth and stones; and wooden men can perhaps be manufactured that will serve the purpose as well. Such command no more respect than men of straw or a lump of dirt.' – *Henry David Thoreau*

Slavery

'We have not abolished slavery; we have nationalised it.' – *Herbert Spencer*

HRT

'Hormone Replacement Therapy (HRT) is the most egregious example of useless and dangerous treatments favoured by stupid doctors. Hormone Replacement Therapy was invented by the drug industry as a way of making money out of a natural event. Time and time again it has been shown to be as dangerous as you might expect it would be – including causing cancer. Women who take HRT have been conned by the drug industry – aided and abetted by the media.' – *Daphne Braithwaite*

Memories

Cats have better memories than dogs, and sheep can remember the faces of 50 other sheep and ten humans for up to two years.

Influencers

Here are three things I have learned about 'influencers'. First, Influencers are intrinsically dishonest since all they have to sell is their influence. If they criticise a product they won't be hired again. Second, I suspect that some 'influencers' online would strip naked and eat themselves alive to push up their ratings. Third, if and when they grow up, influencers become lobbyists. And it is lobbyists who decide national policies. Lobbyists working for drug companies, arms manufacturers, builders and so on control every decision made at national and local level. There are countless thousands of lobbyists based at the European Union headquarters and if you throw a stone in Washington it will probably hit a lobbyist.

Freya Stark

'What did the brassiere say to the top hat?' asked Freya Stark, when talking to the British Ambassador in Cairo in 1942. The Ambassador didn't know. 'You go on ahead, while I give these two a lift,' explained Stark. The Ambassador was reported to have been shocked.

The Old

'The elderly are much more conscious of death because they have touched it, smelt it and felt its cold fingers on their spines. The young know (with enviable certainty) that they are immortal and indestructible.' – *Jack King*

Democracy

'Democracy and socialism have nothing in common but one word – equality. But notice the difference; while democracy seeks equality in liberty, socialism seeks equality in restraint and servitude.' – *Alexis de Tocquerville*

Socialists
'The socialists believe in two things which are absolutely different and perhaps even contradictory: freedom and organisation.' – *Elie Halevy*

David Ogilvy
David Ogilvy, the advertising guru, reckoned that he knew three things worth passing on. First, never lend money to friends. Second, always carry matches. Third, never complain in a restaurant before you have finished your meal.

Kindness
There are still many kind people around. I made a video in which I reported that our central heating had broken. Our house was so cold that I recorded the video wearing a duffle coat, a scarf, a hat and a pair of gloves. I wasn't joking. I was shivering. Within hours I had received an email from someone in New Zealand offering to lend us a property in Georgia, an email from a couple inviting us to share a house in Scotland and a message from a Danish heating engineer offering to fly to England to mend our boiler.

Cheque Mate
A 21-year-old student was shortlisted for an international prize. His work consisted of two cheques (each for £1,000) made out to the two judges.

The Best Headline
'You have 15 days left' is the best newspaper headline I've seen. The '15 days left' is short enough to be scary but long enough for the readers to forget they read it when nothing happens to justify the fear-making words.

Transgendered women in chess
I was surprised to read that transgender women are to be banned from chess tournaments for women. This is curious. Transgender women are banned from athletic competitions and team sports because it is recognised that men are stronger and faster than women.

Are the chess bosses really suggesting that men are intrinsically brainier than women? That's what it sounds like to me. Or, if women find that they are disadvantaged because moving the chess pieces around is too strenuous for them, couldn't someone make lighter chess pieces for women to use?

Paper Tissues
Here is a tip I offer to nurses working in hospitals: When you are about to give bad news to a patient don't walk into the room carrying a box of paper tissues. And if you must do this, do not put the box down beside the patient before you speak.

Triage
I suspect everyone knows the concept of triage. First used in military hospitals, it is now common practice in all forms of medicine. In general practice and hospitals, completely untrained receptionists practise a bastardised version of triage; deciding whether Miss X's chest pains are more worthy of an urgent appointment than Mr Y's chest pains. In Britain, these untrained individuals then decide

whether a patient will be seen in an hour, a day, a week or never.

When practised properly, by Florence Nightingale (who introduced triage in the Crimean War), or by an experienced surgeon in a MASH unit, triage is valuable. But when practised by 18-year-old receptionists who have certificates in domestic science and who don't know or care which end of a stethoscope goes where, it is intrusive and deadly dangerous.

How to Breathe on Television
When talking on television or radio, experienced broadcasters pause for breath in all the wrong places – and never at the end of a sentence. This ensures that they can speak for as long as they like because any interruptions appear rude.

Shopping
In the days before such things became inappropriate, and probably illegal, it was customary (and considered harmless fun) for staff members to welcome new apprentices by sending them to the stores to pick up a jar of elbow grease, a bubble for a spirit level and a gallon of dehydrated water.

Global warming
I wish global warming were real. If we all had warmer winters, far fewer old people would die of the cold.

Trouble
'When trouble is sensed well in advance it can easily be remedied; if you wait for it to show itself any medicine will be too late because the disease will have become incurable. As the doctors say of a

wasting disease, to start with it is easy to cure but difficult to diagnose; after a time, unless it has been diagnosed and treated at the outset, it becomes easy to diagnose but difficult to cure.' – *Niccolo Machiavelli*

Government
'It is every day becoming more clearly understood that the function of government is negative and restrictive, rather than positive and active.' – *Samuel Smiles*

Rules about Art
'In an art gallery, to avoid deep lasting embarrassment, remember that all the questions you were about to ask should remain unspoken. Remember that anything which looks as if it was done by a five-year-old probably could have been done by a five-year-old but will be very expensive. And never forget that no one who teaches art for a living knows anything about Art.' – *Alphonse Monet*

Boutique Hotels
'If you've ever wondered what a boutique hotel is – it's what used to be known as a boarding house.' – *Gerald Smith*

Waiting
In Switzerland, everyone who attends an Accident & Emergency department is seen within 15 minutes at the most. There would be riots and questions asked if anyone ever had to wait 16 minutes. In Britain, where there is a State controlled, publicly funded health care system, patients regularly wait 15 hours to be seen. And waiting times measured in days are not unknown. It is not unknown for

patients to die while waiting to be seen. The trouble is that in the UK, health care is all about waiting. No one seems to realise that all the waiting produces stress, which is bad for the immune system. And it interferes with sleep which is also bad for the immune system. Jean Paul Sartre showed (in The Wall) just how devastating it can be if you mix worry and waiting. Eventually all men go mad. Nevertheless, all health care in Britain is all about waiting these days. Why do doctors and nurses always assume that no one's time is as important as theirs? There is waiting to see the receptionist, waiting to see the nurse, waiting to see the doctor and waiting for results. Why does it take weeks or months to receive the results of a blood test, a tissue sample test or an X-ray? I don't know of any other country in the world where waiting is an integral part of medicine. In Britain, patients must wait for an appointment to be seen, wait to be seen, wait for an appointment to have tests done, wait for the tests to be done and then wait for the results of the tests. And then, of course, they must wait for any treatment they may need. The waiting is accepted by everyone (patients, doctors and nurses) because it is usual. But it is only usual in Britain. Patients in other countries are accustomed to getting tests done on their first appointment and getting their test results given to them within hours at most. And outside Britain, patients who have symptoms are investigated promptly and treated promptly. It is the waiting which has caused Britain to have the worst cancer survival rates in Europe. And no one working in health care seems to understand that waiting exacerbates the natural and inevitable fear of the unknown, and that fear of the unknown is the greatest fear of all.

Prophet

Back in the 1970s I had a posh literary agent (Anne McDermid of Curtis Brown – one of the best known literary agencies in the world). She warned me that I was a prophet crying in the wilderness. It is now clear that she was absolutely correct. I was. And I still am.

Sticky Beer

Beer tasters in Olde England would pour some ale onto a bench. Wearing leather trousers a taster would sit on the damp patch for thirty minutes and then stand up. If his trousers stuck to the bench, the publican would be fined for serving beer that contained too much sugar. It's probably not a good idea to try this in your local hostelry.

Rabbits

We feed the squirrels in our garden every day. They come bounding up to the house if we call them. We buy bagsful of walnuts and hazelnuts for them. In addition to feeding the birds and the squirrels, we have started feeding carrots to the rabbits in our garden. Out of habit rather than for any other reason, we put the fresh carrots down on an area of grass between the greenhouse and one of the bird feeders. The rabbits have become accustomed to their daily treats, and every morning they run up to see what has been put out for them. If there is nothing there they turn round, stare look at the hedge on the other side of the lawn and pretend that they are simply staring into space. Then they turn round to see what Father Christmas has brought. Sadly, the carrots we have delivered every Friday from our local supermarket are usually rotten before the following Wednesday so I'm growing their Wednesday and Thursday carrots in the greenhouse. For obvious reasons, I can't grow the carrots in the garden.

Lunatics

'The lunatics who have taken over the asylum want to stop all mining and drilling, and they're doing everything they can to ensure that mining companies and oil companies can't raise the money that is needed to start a new mine. I wonder how many of the lunatics know that you can't build an electric car or a windmill or a solar panel without digging tons of 'stuff' out of the earth. And I wonder how many realise that, on average, it takes 23 years from discovering a new mineral source to digging stuff out of the ground.'

– Jack King

The Day I Nearly Joined MI5

'A few months ago, I saw an advertisement from MI5. They were looking for a new Chief Scientific Advisor. I couldn't resist it. I obtained an application form and filled it in. It was all terribly casual though they did tell me I shouldn't tell anyone I'd applied. (So don't tell anyone I told you.) I sent in an e-mail request for a form and it occurred to me afterwards that the people at MI5 who routinely read my e-mails must have had something close to a fit when they saw it.

When I told The Princess I had applied for a job at MI5, she misheard and wanted to know why I'd applied for a job with a furniture superstore. 'There are two things I don't understand,' she said. 'Why do you want a job with MFI and why can't I tell anyone?' I told her I couldn't answer either question.

When the form arrived I filled it in very neatly. I gave them the Post Box address, of course. Either they know where we really live (in which case they don't need to be told) or they don't (in which case I'm not going to tell them and they're so incompetent that they don't deserve to know anyway). On the form they seemed more concerned about whether I had any disabilities than anything else. They asked three times and in the end, because I felt that I wasn't likely to be taken seriously unless I could tell them about some disablement, I made something up. I can't remember what it was now so if anyone ever finds the form and asks me about it I'll be in a tricky position.

Going through my accumulated e-mails I see that I haven't got the job.

I wasn't terribly disappointed or surprised.

Antoinette said she wondered if it was because they thought I was too old and asked if I thought I should take them to an industrial tribunal. The thought did appeal but somehow I expect I'll forget about it and never get round to doing anything. It would be a jolly wheeze, though.

It did occur to me this afternoon that if they had any sense they would have hired me. A bit of imagination and lateral thinking wouldn't have done them any harm.' – *Taken from 'Diary of a Disgruntled Man' by Vernon Coleman*

Rich
'He who knows when he has got enough is rich.' – *Lao Tzu*

Why you?
In a film called 'An Affair to Remember' starring Cary Grant and Deborah Kerr, the two are due to meet at the top of the Empire State Building but the woman played by Deborah Kerr is crippled on the way to the rendezvous and cannot keep the date. Grant's line, when he finds out, is seared into my heart. 'If it had to happen to one of us,' he says, 'why did it have to be you?'

Clausewitz
Clausewitz, the legendary German military author pointed out that it is never sensible to make your plans according to what your enemy might do, or intends to do, but only according to what he can do.

John Wick
The only way to survive is to live day to day, one hour at a time, and to try to find love and peace where they hide. And, to quote a line from the film John Wick 3: 'If you want peace prepare for war'.

Cliff edge
Having cancer is like living on the edge of a crumbling cliff.

A Way
Either I will find a way or make one.
From a family crest which had a pickaxe on it.

The Worst Inventions of the last 100 years
Barbie Dolls
Social Media
Electric cars
Trousers for women
Cosmetic surgery
Speed cameras
Tights for women
Artificial Intelligence
Cameras on cycle helmets
Computers
The Internet
24 Hours News Programmes on television

Legislation
'The value of legislation as an agent in human advancement has usually been much over-estimated.' – *Samuel Smiles*

Civilisation
'We were the first to assert that the more complicated the forms of civilisation, the more restricted the freedom of the individual must become.' – *Benito Mussolini*

Just a Nudge

There are several hundred nudge units being run by governments around the world. These nudge units (offering what is sometimes called libertarian paternalism but which is in reality a psy-op designed to fool people into behaving the way the Government wants them to behave) aim to trick people into behaving in a way that the Government thinks will improve their lives. The principle behind this psychological trickery is that people don't make the right decisions and need to be nudged into doing what is best for them, and everyone else. So, for example, instead of allowing workers to choose to enrol in a pension scheme, the British Government now insists that workers must be enrolled in a pension scheme unless they opt out. The workers have been nudged into behaving sensibly. We are all now being constantly nudged this way and that way. It's all part of the process of driving us into the overall scheme known as 'social credit'.

Radon

Whatever happened to the threat posed by radon? Back in the 1980s, homeowners were all told to check their homes for radon poisoning – even though, in truth, the risks seemed to me to be somewhere between minute and not worth worrying about. Those said to be at risk were encouraged to spend thousands of pounds protecting their homes and themselves against the danger posed by radon. Much to everyone's surprise, building companies were enthusiastic about the radon testing programme. Today, radon testing is a fringe industry; a leftover scare still struggling for visibility.

Ignorance

'The truth is that our race survived ignorance; it is our scientific genius that will do us in.' – *Stephen Vizinczey*

Your Body has a complex early warning

'Your body has a whole range of special early warning sy:
These are designed to give you advance notice of any prot
which seem likely to arise and to ensure that potential damage is
kept to a minimum.

For example, if your heart is under too much strain and the small vessels which supply it with blood are not able to pump in fluid at a fast enough rate, you will start to suffer chest pains. These pains, usually known as angina, are not in themselves life-threatening. Nor do they suggest that there is any desperately serious life-threatening disorder present. You are being told that your heart has reached its limits and that if you want to avoid any further damage you must make some adjustments to your way of life. You must either change your eating and exercise habits so that your heart can enjoy a better blood supply or you must reduce its workload.

Angina is probably one of the best-known early warning signs of physical distress, but there are many others. Indigestion, for example, is nothing more than an indication that your stomach is finding it difficult to cope with the quality and quantity of food that you're putting into it. Muscle cramps that come on during exercise are an early sign intended to show you that your muscles are using up oxygen and food faster than fresh supplies are being provided.

Although many of the most obvious early warning signs relate to specific physical illnesses, there are also those which are intended to tell you when your body is run down and when you are in genuine need of a rest. When the problem is a general one, the signs will usually appear as a whole series of apparently trivial ailments. You may suddenly find that you are getting lots of coughs and colds, or that you are suffering from spots and boils.

Just as the body can get tired and may show early signs of physical distress, so the mind can become world weary and may need a break from the daily pressures. For example, you may feel lethargic, off-colour or generally out-of-sorts – all these vague symptoms may suggest that you have been pushing yourself too hard. If you are unusually irritable or impulsive, if your memory begins to fail you, if you can't get to sleep, if you become intolerant of noise, if your ability to concentrate seems to have gone or if your willpower seems to have disappeared, if you find yourself crying, overreacting and unable to deal with trivial tasks, the chances are high that you have been doing too much. Your mind needs a rest.

Many people do recognise that these are all signs of overwork and excess pressure, but find themselves unable to do anything constructive to help themselves because they feel guilty if they stop working. Those of us who refuse to listen to these simple warning signs and to take notice of our bodies when they tell us to take things easy for a while, should perhaps remember that some of the greatest men and women the world has ever known happily cut themselves off from all outside contacts whenever they felt themselves to be under too much pressure. Charles Darwin used to pretend to be physically ill in order to give himself a chance to rest in bed whenever he felt himself to be under too much strain. So did Florence Nightingale, Marcel Proust, Sigmund Freud and many others.

Carried to excess, this type of behaviour may well be described as malingering. Employed with care and thought, it is more accurately described as common sense.

Most of us have a weak point. When we are under too much stress or too much pressure we develop symptoms of a particular type. Learn to know your weak point – as the symptoms begin to develop, you'll know that you are pushing yourself too hard.

Here are some of the commonest 'weak point' signs:
* Headache
* Skin rash
* Indigestion
* Wheezing
* Diarrhoea
* Chest pains
* Palpitations
* Insomnia
* Irritability

All of them show that you are beginning to suffer actual physical damage as a result of the stress to which you have exposed yourself. Your stress threshold has been reached.

Spot your own weak point and act on the warning it provides.' – *(Taken from 'Bodypower' by Vernon Coleman)*

Statism
'In a country where the sole employer is the State, oppo death by slow starvation. The old principle; who does not work shall not eat, has been replaced by a new one: who does not obey shall not eat.' – *Leon Trotsky*

Desperation
'The mass of men lead lives of quiet desperation.' – *Henry David Thoreau*

Grammar
'I learned grammar when I was a private soldier on the pay of sixpence a day. The edge of my berth, or that of my guard bed, was my seat to study in; my knapsack was my bookcase; a bit of board lying on my lap was my writing table; and the task did not demand anything like a year of my life. I had no money to purchase a candle or oil; in winter time it was rarely that I could get any evening light but that of the fire, and only my turn even of that. And if I, under such circumstances, and without parent or friend to advise or encourage me, accomplished this undertaking, what excuse can there be for any youth, however poor, however pressed with business, or however circumstanced as to room or other conveniences?' – *William Cobbett*

GPs are Lazy, not Overworked
Modern GPs in the UK are constantly complaining that they are desperately overworked and cannot cope. Doctors' representatives say the same thing. But the evidence proves that GPs are NOT overworked. After all, in 2024, the average GP worked just 23 to 24 hours a week. Most people would regard that as part time work. And

s were paid around £150,000 a year.

Today there are nearly twice as many GPs in England and Wales as there were in 1964 when I started medical school. And if you look at the number of GPs per 100,000 patients, the figures show that there are more GPs available than ever. Back in 1964, there were 42 GPs per 100,000 patients. Today, there are around 60 GPs per 100,000 patients.

And remember that GPs used to do home visits, night calls, weekend calls and calls on bank holidays. It was not uncommon for a GP to see 20 patients in a morning surgery, 20 patients in an evening surgery and do a list of home visits in between. At night and at weekends the doctor would be on call to visit patients at home.

Today, very few GPs do any of those things.

And many GPs refuse to see patients 'live' – insisting on doing their consultations over the phone or the internet, even though the evidence shows that it is impossible to provide proper care for patients without seeing most of them in person. .

Ring a GP's surgery today with an emergency and you will be told to go to hospital. In the bad old days, GPs would visit patients at home 24 hours a day. And would sew up wounds and deal with a whole range of emergencies.

The only possible conclusion is that today's GPs are not overworked. Indeed, they do far less work than their predecessors did decades ago. It's not surprising that hospital Accident and Emergency departments cannot cope.

When I was a GP we worked a damned sight harder than today's doctors. We had responsibility for our patients 24 hours a day, every day of the year. And we took bloods, gave injections and syringed ears without whingeing that these things weren't our responsibility. We put in stitches and then, later, we took them out again.

It seems to me that many of today's GPs don't really care about their patients but seem to be in medicine only for the money. I weep at how general practice has deteriorated. Patients get a terrible deal. Too many doctors seem to me to be lazy and greedy; in medicine only for what they can get out of it. They have no sense of responsibility and no sense of vocation. The latest trend is for GPs to use assistants (who are not medically qualified and whose salaries are largely paid by taxpayers) to see patients on their behalf and do their work for them.

Adulterate
The verb 'to doctor' means 'to adulterate'.

Sticks
I was about to set off two hundred yards down the lane to the post box when Antoinette put a walking stick in my hand. I took it gratefully. Spectacles to read and a stick for walking. Where will it all end, I ask myself. But I do not hear the question because I'm rather deaf.

Barbie
Protestors stole 300 Barbie and Duke dolls from stores in New York, USA and switched their voice boxes. They then put the dolls back on the shelves so that the Barbie dolls snarled 'Eat lead, Cobra' and the macho Duke doll said 'Let's go shopping.'

AI
People get terribly excited about AI but so far it has produced nonsense, made up references and stolen work from professional authors. AI exists only to destroy all the Arts, design, architecture, etc., by providing thieves with an easy opportunity. There are already whole books of my work available under other people's names on the internet. (Curiously, one book of my material was banned when I tried to publish it under my own name. It is rather galling to see that the same platform is allowing someone else to sell my suppressed material quite freely.)

Artificial Intelligence companies have helped themselves to work by thousands of writers and artists and fed the material into databases to enable their customers to create their own 'works of art' simply by telling the software what style of writing or art to copy. The result is that the internet is now awash with fake books and fake art. Add this to the ability, and willingness, of unscrupulous companies to steal the identity of individuals (both their photographs and their voices) and it is clear that the future is awash with opportunities for thieves of all kinds.

The only people who will benefit most from AI are billionaires with huge software companies.

Middle Classes

Traditionally, the middle classes in any society are always the most dangerous. They are usually the most articulate and the most likely to rebel and stand up both for their individual rights, and for what they see as their patriotic responsibilities.

Because of this, the conspirators have taken much care to oppress this group.

The poor who are on benefits of one kind or another (either because they are unemployed or because they consider themselves too ill to work) are not seen as much of a problem for those leading the human race into the Great Reset. They are, after all, already bought and paid for, controlled by the State and ready, willing and able to slide easily and comfortably into a world where the Universal Basic Income is the usual form of payment and has replaced wages, salaries and fees.

Clothes

'No man ever stood the lower in my estimation for having a patch in his clothes; yet I am sure that there is greater anxiety, commonly, to have fashionable, or at least clean and un-patched clothes, than to have a sound conscience.' – *Henry David Thoreau*

Politicians

You would be hard pressed to find anyone who didn't agree with the thought that politicians are out for themselves and care nothing for the electorate or the world around them. Politicians think only of ways to enrich themselves. No modern, professional politician believes in anything or cares about anything. They have no beliefs or ideology. They are in the business of politics because they aren't good at anything else. They are little more than exhibitionists, and it should be no surprise that so many of them end up in prison or on reality television shows. Thanks to our crooked and incompetent politicians, the British government was, in early 2024, spending over 14% of its income on paying interest on its debts (but not paying back the capital). If interest rates remain level then the cost of paying the interest will soon reach 25% of the Government's revenues. Add in the cost of paying pensions to state employees, and there will soon be nothing left to pay for health care, education, road repairs or infrastructure improvements. Other countries have similar figures. In America, the Government's debt is eye watering and will probably never be paid off. Generations ahead are going to pay for the recklessness of current administrations.

Minority

'I find more and more that it is well to be on the side of the minority, since it is always the more intelligent.' – *Goethe*

Civil Servants

'Over a century ago, the British Foreign Office (tasked with looking after an Empire) managed with a dozen or so men of integrity, honour and clarity. Today, the civil service consists, at the top end, of armies of men and women who are constantly looking around for ways in which they can profit from their contacts by jumping to a well-paid job in an international company. Civil servants and quango heads are forever moving between private and public jobs and always thinking first and foremost of themselves. At the bottom end, the civil service is full of men and women whose sole concern is to do the minimum amount of work which will enable them to get through the day.

What is true of national government is also true of local government and it is no surprise that councils everywhere are as badly run as central government. Elected councillors and unelected officials are greedy, overpaid and consumed by their own personal interests, at the expense of the local electorate. It is hardly surprising that many councils around the world are going bust. As with central government, the problem is not a shortage of money but the way the money is spent. Staff working for local councils are paid absurdly high salaries, and given absurdly over-generous pensions. The result is that it won't be long before local taxes will be entirely used up paying the pensions of former executives. It is easy to think that councils are in financial trouble because councillors and executives are incompetent. But that isn't true. It isn't just incompetence (though that plays a part) which is destroying the financial stability of local government – but corruption.' – *Jack King*

Pain

The mainstream media has published claims that people who take opioid painkillers are much at risk of becoming addicted. This is nonsense. A study involving 148 pieces of research (involving 4.3 million adult chronic pain sufferers) showed that less than 1 in 10 developed dependence or opioid use disorder. And even that figure is too high. The Faculty of Pain Medicine at the Royal College of Anaethetists says: 'It is rare for people in pain to become addicted to opioids.'

Problems arise when patients are given painkillers which they don't really need. And often patients aren't told how to take their painkillers.

So why all the scary publicity?

I fear that the media scares are being used as an excuse for doctors to prescribe fewer painkillers. The scares are also being used to reduce palliative care and to promote euthanasia.

Where did all the news go?

There is no news any more. Or, rather, there undoubtedly is news' – but we don't get to find out about it. Newspapers, magazines, television and radio don't report the news in the way that the news was reported a few decades ago, because today's journalists insist on producing what can only accurately be described as propaganda. Everything that looks like a news story is presented with a slant which fits the attitude and prejudices of the writer. The reason there is no news is that there are no journalists these days – just leader writers and feature writers. The BBC in particular is a disgrace and I honestly don't think the organisation employs anyone whom I would describe as a 'journalist' or who would have held down a job on any publication, however small, a few decades ago.

Since mainstream publishers fired most of their older journalists some years ago, the field has been left open for young, inexperienced and constantly opinionated left wing journalists to take over. The vast majority of young journalists are left wing liberals who believe everything they are told to believe, and are consequently firmly committed in the perils of climate change. The news about climate change, wars, health issues and whatever else is constantly biased. It is nigh on impossible for the average reader, who relies upon the mainstream media for news about what is going on in the world, to hear anything other than very one-sided propaganda.

Sadly, and rather surprisingly, seemingly intelligent, informed people cannot see that there are too many 'coincidences'. They prefer not even to suspect that there could be malevolent forces at work and so they close their ears and eyes to obvious truths, label the worriers and truth-tellers as conspiracy theorists, and are content when the authorities demonise and silence the truth tellers.

Life

'Do not fear death so much, but rather the inadequate life.' – *Bertolt Brecht*

Abraham Lincoln
Abraham Lincoln had many failures when running for office. He lost his first attempt to become an Illinois State legislator in 1832. He lost races for House Speaker in 1836 and 1838. He lost at his first attempt to become a congressman in 1843. In 1849, he was beaten in an attempt to become a land officer in Illinois. He lost an election for the US Senate in 1854 and was defeated in an attempt to become vice president in 1856. He failed again to enter the Senate in 1858. Also, in 1833, his grocery business failed. He did not finish paying off the debts until 1848. But he became US President in 1860. Five years later he was shot.

Hopeful
'To be seventy years young is sometimes far more cheerful and hopeful than to be forty years old.' – *Oliver Wendell Holmes*

Complaints
'The only way to communicate with any government department, utility or large corporation is to make a formal complaint. Endless legislation ensures that formal complaints must be taken seriously and you will usually be honoured with an individual reply. If you then ooze sweetness and light and imply that your complaint will be dropped if the source of your dissatisfaction is dealt with immediately (or at least forthwith) then you have a good chance of obtaining an acceptable outcome. The temptation of being able to put you down as a complainant who has been attended to satisfactorily will be too great for the organisation to resist.' – *Marc Charbonnier*

Banned
Many of my books have been banned. I would rather my books were burned than banned. If copies are available to be burned then at least the book must have been published.

The Office for Budget Responsibility Speaks
Britain's Office for Budget Responsibility (which sounds as if it were invented by George Orwell) has said that population growth has led to a decline in living standards in Britain. Well, shiver my timbers, what a shock. A six-year-old could have worked that out. What the 'experts' are effectively saying is that if you have a house with six people living in it, and then another six people move into the house, but without bringing in more money, then the living standards of the original six will fall. There will be less money for food, energy or repairs. It is, of course, exactly, what many of us have been saying for decades. (Incidentally, the OBR has a staff of 45 civil servants and has a Budget Responsibility Committee, an Oversight Board, an Advisory Panel and a Think-tank Roundtable.) The only mystery is why a bunch of no doubt well-paid experts would expose themselves to so much sniggering by stating the obvious. The only explanation I can think of is that they didn't realise that what they were saying would have been obvious to a six-year-old. And that is worrying.

Denial
After the end of World War II it was difficult to find any Germans who would admit to having supported Hitler – and yet there is a good deal of film showing Hitler being applauded by huge crowds of Germans. Similarly, after four years of lies about covid and the covid vaccine, it was difficult to find any doctor who thought that giving the experimental covid vaccine to billions of people was a good idea – and yet thousands of doctors gave the vaccine and told their nurses to give it. And the compliant, unthinking doctors made a good deal of money doing so.

Parking

Hospital car parks are always far too small and so there are always queues of cars driving around, their drivers desperately looking for spaces. There is invariably one car, nearly always an Audi of some kind, parked in such a way as to occupy two spaces. Why does that always produce such anger? And in the hospital we visit most often there is a fair amount of scrap wasteland in the middle of the car park. It could easily be converted into a small garden so that patients or relatives could sit while waiting. Or, more usefully, it could be used to extend the car park. Instead, however, there is a wooden fence around it to prevent people trespassing. Traffic wardens patrol the car park to hand out tickets. I actually saw a traffic warden put a payment notice onto the windscreen of a car which had just overrun its time by one minute. What sort of person takes a job as a traffic warden in a hospital car park?

It cost £8.50 to park the car for a standard length visit. The hospital operates a park and ride service (£2 each way on a bus) but the idea of expecting a patient to travel on a bus to a car park after day case surgery is obscene.

Oddly enough, the car park machine advises that motorists can park for 20 minutes free of charge. What the hell can you do at the hospital that takes only 20 minutes? You could, I suppose, park, run to the hospital entrance and then run back to the car.

Inevitably, it is often nigh on impossible to find a parking space at our local hospital. (When I say 'local' I really mean nearest. It takes an hour to drive there. Smaller, genuinely local hospitals have been closed in the surge to centralisation.) Patients have to arrive before dawn to find a space because most of the spaces are taken up with staff cars. Tired of driving round and round looking for a space, I have had an official looking metal sign made for our truck. The sign says: NOTICE: MAINTENANCE ON SITE and I shall park on the grass and place the sign on the inside of the windscreen next time we're at the hospital. Naughty? Probably. But only if you have spent an hour desperately looking for a parking space in a hospital car park in order to meet a timed radiotherapy appointment can you possibly know the extent of the frustration that can drive a man to such things.

People's behaviour can become primitive when they're desperate to find a car park space. After her operation I had to borrow a wheelchair to take Antoinette to the car. She was still semi-conscious with her pulse irregular and very fast. As I helped her into the front seat, a woman driver from another car came towards us. I thought for a moment that she was coming to see if she could help.

'Are you leaving?' she demanded.

'In a few moments,' I answered, as I struggled with Antoinette. She was grey and looked like death.

'Why in a few moments?' demanded the woman. She was standing just a few feet away and could see perfectly well that I was struggling to get Antoinette seated.

I fitted the seat belt around Antoinette and ignored the woman. I wanted to shout at her but am still quite proud that I refrained; realising that this would probably result in a delay to our journey home.

Car park Joy

At the end of one radiotherapy session we went back to the car and found an elderly couple in their car cruising around looking for a space. They were overjoyed when we told them that we were leaving. The woman gave Antoinette a big hug of thanks. 'I'm so happy I could kiss you!' she said, with tears in her eyes. The man just kept saying 'thank you, thank you'. There is something seriously wrong with the system when a frail, elderly couple attending a hospital can be so grateful just because they have found somewhere to dump their car. The hospital should ban hospital staff from parking at the hospital (and make them use an offsite parking area with a bus service) or they should build a multi storey car park (which would doubtless pay for its construction in a month). Antoinette and I now have an agreement. If I can't find a car parking space then she will go to into the hospital to keep whatever appointment she has and I will join her when I have dumped the car.

Liberty and Safety
'Those who would give up essential liberty, to purchase a little temporary safety, deserve neither liberty nor safety.' – *Benjamin Franklin*

Gift
There is a wonderful moment in the television film of The Perfect Spy when the character known as Poppy gives Magnus a copy of a book called *Simplicissimus*. It is clearly a valued, well-thumbed copy.
   'This is your own copy,' says Magnus, surprised.
   'Would you rather I gave you something that was not of value to me?' replies Poppy.

Castro
Castro didn't take power in Cuba because of the Russians. It was big American companies which put him in power (particularly those associated with hotels and casinos). The people who backed Castro thought they'd get a better deal from him than from Batista. And for a while they probably did.

God
There are certain themes which always seems popular with publishers. And so authors regularly produce books claiming that there is no God. And such books always seem to do well; nice little pot boilers earning ready money for the cynical, who are ever-ready to thumb their noses at faith in the interests of serving mammon. All you have to do is to challenge believers to prove that there is a God, and then, since they obviously won't be able to do this, announce

with glee that your hypothesis is proven. I have never truly understood the absurd arrogance of these people. Why do they do this when religion may have been dismissed by Marx as the opium of the people but still offers comfort? Denying the existence of God (and claiming to know that there is no God when there is no way they can prove the non-existence of God) is utterly pointless and unutterably cruel to those who gain comfort from the existence of a higher being. Patients with cancer and other serious disorders often rely on their God. As do people in many other circumstances – including simply the elderly, the lonely and the generally fearful. Belief in a higher being gives comfort and strengthens hope. Who the hell is anyone to try to squash hope? That is an evil thing to do.

Sick Google

After my wife, Antoinette, was diagnosed with breast cancer she did a web search using the Google search engine, looking for soft bras for breast cancer sufferers who had just had surgery. She immediately started to receive advertisements for funeral services. And within hours she was being inundated with advertisements for cremation services. Other people get ads for shoes, cars or frocks. Patients struggling to cope with cancer diagnoses get ads for cremation services, funeral directors and cut price deals on coffins. It is comical to think that when Google was formed its founders were said to have claimed that their aim was 'to do no evil'.

Decline

Societies go into decline because they become too complicated. Politicians and bureaucrats respond to every small problem with a new law (they call some of them rules and regulations but if you can be punished for not doing something then the rule or regulation might as well be called a law as far as I'm concerned) and every new law makes life more complicated. Each new law requires time and energy and expense. And so life gets increasingly unbearable. This increase in complexity can be seen in everything we touch, but few things illustrate the problem more effectively than motor cars. We used to own a beautiful Maserati but eventually we just had to sell it because it was so complicated that I found it frightening, unfriendly and demanding. There was a touch screen computer on the Maserati's dashboard, though I never understood how it worked. The satellite navigation system was excellent when I could press the right buttons to turn it on, but the only way I could manage to turn off the radio was to turn on the hands free telephone button. Since I don't have a hands free telephone device, the button simply turned off the radio. I found this to be a useful trick for when the car came back from a service with the radio blaring away. The 91-page quick reference guide (a supplement to the handbook) informed me that I should look out for 62 different little warning lights which would tell me that something was wrong or going wrong. In addition to all the usual warning signs (a seat belt isn't fastened, the parking brake is on, the oil pressure is low) there were incomprehensive hieroglyphics to tell me that the tyre pressure was low (the car would tell me which tyre has low pressure and precisely what the pressure was for that tyre and all the other tyres); that there was water in the fuel supply; that the headlight aiming system was malfunctioning; that there was ice outside, that the brake pads were becoming worn; that I had exceeded the speed limit; that the AWD was malfunctioning (I don't have the foggiest what that is) and that the AdBlue levels were low (ditto). There were warning lights to tell me that the FCW was malfunctioning, that the LKA was malfunctioning and that the BSA was malfunctioning. Oh and did I mention that there is one to tell me that the AWD is malfunctioning? I did? Oh good. There was a suspension malfunction indicator and an ADAS status indicator which appears only to provide 'examples with only LKA activated and LKA-ACC systems activated'. And on and on and on it went – pages and pages of incomprehensible drivel. And I always had a suspicion that information about my driving was being constantly reported to the police. Moreover, the Maserati had so much electric stuff going on all the time that the battery was constantly running down. To avoid problems, the battery had to be connected to the mains every 14 days or so. And here's the killer: the battery was stored in the boot and I could only open the boot by using a button on the key. I was well aware that if the battery went flat the only way to get at the battery would be to find a small and agile mechanic who was prepared, and able, to remove the back seats and climb into the boot. Our 67-year-old Bentley, our pride and joy, also keeps its battery in the boot but when the ignition is switched off that's it. The car shuts down until I need it again. And if I should, for example, want to open a window with the engine switched off then I just use the appropriate handle and wind down the window. If the Bentley's battery does go flat and needs attention I simply open the boot, with a small, metal object called a key, and either replace the battery or attach some jump leads. Incidentally, we needed new batteries for the Bentley and for the Maserati. The new battery for the Maserati cost £398.80 and we were charged £117.00 to have the battery fitted. The total cost of the new, huge battery for the Bentley (including the cost of fitting it) was £105.50.

Dreams
'Life is a dream. It's waking up that kills us.' – *Virginia Woolf*

The Machines
Self-drive cars might still be some time away (particularly in countries such as Britain where the roads are often narrow and with blind bends) but cars are taking over. For example, cars now sold in Europe have to be fitted with Intelligent Speed Assistance which will tell the driver if he is ignoring the speed limit. If he ignores the warning then the car will slow down anyway. The driver will have no choice. I am delighted to report that our 1957 Bentley S1 is not fitted with anything quite so intrusive. (Mind you, it isn't fitted with seat belts either. And I don't have to pay a road fund licence or take it to an MOT garage once a year.)

Face Masks
During the covid nonsense, Professor Susan Michie, a communist, a psychologist and one of the scientists advising the British

Government, said that the measures introduced to tackle the coronavirus pandemic should be retained to help suppress other viruses and boost public health. She recommended that people should wear face masks forever and that people should check that they had a face mask with them when they left home, in the same way that they made an effort to remember their phone and keys. I found, and still find, this advice to be curious and rather alarming since medical evidence shows not only that face masks provide little or no protection but that they cause many serious physical and mental health problems. I can't help feeling that Professor Michie's advice owed more to her membership of the communist party than to any medical knowledge she might have.

Post Codes

While sorting through old paperwork, I found details of a campaign I joined countless decades ago to oppose the introduction of post codes on addresses. There is now no doubt that post codes (aka zip codes) were the first sign of 'them' taking control, and the first sign that we were losing our privacy and, indeed, our humanity. Every day, the reach of Big Brother delves deeper into our lives. The police in the UK will now be able to run face recognition searches based on the photos on 50 million driving licences. (There will be thousands of errors since driving licence photos, like passport photos, are laughably unrecognisable.) And if you want to travel abroad now you will have to be photographed and finger printed – just like a criminal. You will need a visa to go anywhere in Europe and to almost anywhere else in the world. Indeed, it is difficult to avoid the suspicion that in the eyes of the authorities we are all criminals now.

Delivering what?

Why do so many delivery companies insist on having phone numbers and email addresses before they will deliver a parcel? With this information (together with the name of the addressee and their address) their staff can easily steal an individual's identity. I had my identity stolen some years ago. It wasn't a fun experience

B12 Deficiency

Antoinette suffered from neurological problems for 10 years. She had been depressed and had thought constantly of suicide. She saw her GP, visited an expensive but very dismissive and rather supercilious private neurologist and was thoroughly investigated at the Frenchay Hospital near Bristol. Doctors there had at one point suggested a diagnosis of motor neurone disease. Multiple sclerosis had been another possibility.

But all the neurologists had missed the diagnosis of vitamin B12 deficiency which was the real cause of Antoinette's problems.

Sadly, this isn't unusual.

Astonishingly, 14% of patients wait at least 10 years for a diagnosis of B12 deficiency. Antoinette had all signs and symptoms of MS because the symptoms caused by B12 deficiency are pretty much identical. In both disorders the problems are caused by demyelination.

In the UK, it is regarded as normal if a patient has B12 levels which are over 180. In Europe and Japan, the 'normal' figure is 550. It is well accepted that patients can develop B12 deficiency symptoms if their blood levels are below 400. It seems likely that there are tens, if not hundreds, of thousands of sufferers in Britain whose serious problems could be cured with nothing more than regular injections of vitamin B12.

When Antoinette was eventually, belatedly, diagnosed with vitamin B12 deficiency (known to people with medical degrees – or a possibly unhealthy obsession with matters medical – as sub-acute combined degeneration of the cord) she was prescribed regular injections of B12 because her intestines don't absorb the vitamin properly. We have, however, proved to our satisfaction that tablets taken sublingually (put under the tongue) are absorbed perfectly well and produce a better response than painful and far more expensive injections. (When I was beginning to show signs of vitamin B12 deficiency I had myself tested. The results showed a marginal result which my GP didn't think worth treating. I took sublingual B12 once a week and my symptoms disappeared. The test done in the UK for B12 deficiency is woeful and can be dangerously misleading.)

Tyranny

Rule by bureaucrats gives us tyranny without a tyrant. When no one is responsible there can be no justice and no freedom.

Oxygen

There is an assumption (widespread among the medical profession as well as the public) that you cannot have too much of some things – such as oxygen. This is nonsense, of course. Too much oxygen can be deadly.

Consider the following paragraph taken from my book *Why and How Doctors kill more people than Cancer*.

My father was in hospital.

'I was allowed to visit because he had suddenly become very ill. When I visited him I found that he was very pink, confused and twitching. When he did wake up he had difficulty in seeing. He was on oxygen and it seemed pretty clear to me that he was getting too much of the stuff and was suffering from oxygen poisoning. These are all classic symptoms of this problem. I asked for the oxygen to be stopped. The oxygen was stopped and the following morning my father was fine.'

The ward was stuffed with doctors and nurses. Why did no one notice? My father would have died if the oxygen had not been stopped.

And sometimes oxygen is deliberately used with terrible results.

Consider this paragraph, taken from my book *The Medicine Men* (written in 1975):

'Other researchers have deliberately blinded children when studying the effects of oxygen on blindness of new-born children. Clinical observation suggested that newly-born children given high concentrations of oxygen became blind, and to prove this point, three separate studies were performed in America in the early 1950s. A total of twenty-seven children were deliberately blinded.'

Forums

Online forums set up so that patients can exchange information do more harm than good because the majority of those who use such sites only write about the bad things that have happened to them and many exaggerate and dramatise their experiences. There are even rather sad individuals who seem to want to boast that their condition is worse than anyone else's. It is easy to drift downwards in a spiral of fear and despair – both of which cause massive physical and mental damage to those using the site.

Research

Surprisingly, little really useful medical research is done these days because all research is drug company related. And it has been clear for decades that research which produces inconvenient or commercially threatening results is suppressed.

Flat feet

Policemen (and it was mainly or only men in those days) used to walk the streets. Their very flat-footed presence prevented much crime and ensured that people could walk around safely. Then the police started to sit in cars parked on motorway bridges because bosses realised that you could increase your arrests by targeting motorists (who rarely carry guns or knives and are an easy target) instead of trying to prevent crime or arrest criminals. And all those fines meant that policing became profitable. Now things have changed again and today the police spend most of their time sitting at desks staring at computer screens. They trawl the internet looking for comments which might prove offensive to someone, somewhere. It is not surprising, perhaps, that polls show that in the UK 0% of the public believe that the police do a good job.

More worrying still, in the last three years the police have failed to solve any burglaries in half of England and Wales. Burglary has become a 'no risk' crime in much of the country. Shoplifters are ignored by the police. Meanwhile, a scary number of policemen have been arrested for assault, sex crimes and murder and an annoying large amount of police time is still wasted on surfing the web looking for alleged extremists. (The new definition of 'extremist' appears to be 'someone who tells the truth'.)

The vast majority of crimes in Britain which do not involve motorists are not investigated. The vast majority of crimes which are investigated do not result in an arrest. (Only 5.6% of crimes lead to a charge, let alone an arrest or a sentence.) And nearly 10% of all serious offences (including violence, sex crimes, possession of weapons and theft) result in the offender being expected to apologise for their misbehaviour but not serving any sort of sentence. These crimes are not recorded and so the 'criminals' do not have a criminal record and the crime figures are kept artificially low.

Early Retirement

Several million Britons who have only just passed their 50th birthdays have chosen to retire, exhausted by a battle with life that they feel they have lost. Another couple of million who haven't yet reached their 30th birthdays have given up too – beaten before they've started, and choosing the lazy way out. A few retain dreams that they will one day become YouTube or TikTok stars, or influencers but on the whole most seem to be suffering from chronic ergophobia.

Most of these people expect the state to provide them with food, heating and accommodation. Very few have enough money, or big enough pensions, to enable them to live independently. Just how sensible they are to retire early is a tricky question. It's true that they might have more time to play golf and travel but will the benefits they receive from the state be sufficient to enable them to do anything other than spend an hour on the local crazy golf course and have a day trip to the seaside? I doubt it. Most will spend their days watching daytime television and doing puzzles in magazines and newspapers (all of which now provide special puzzle supplements to satisfy this demand). How many people will feel satisfied without the framework of daily work and the thrill of a job well done? For most people, retirement will end up as an endless desert of time-filling. The result will be that the boredom and lack of satisfaction will result in early deaths. Activity keeps us alert (both physically and mentally) and an early retirement will too often lead to an early death.

Thoughts on Life and the Other Thing
1. 'Life is slow dying.' – Philip Larkin
2. 'May no new thing arise.' – Patrick O'Brian
3. 'No one here gets out alive.' – Jim Morrison
4. 'All of life is 6 to 5 against.' – Damon Runyon
5. 'It's not over till it's over.' – Yogi Berra
6. 'Do not go gently into that good night' – Dylan Thomas
7. 'There is only one solution if old age is not to be an absurd parody of our former life, and that is to go on pursuing ends that give our existence a meaning – devotion to individuals, to groups or to causes – social, political, intellectual or creative work.' – Simone de Beauvoir
8. 'Life is like playing a solo in public and learning the instrument as you go along,' – Samuel Butler.
9. 'I remember about thirty times a day between waking and sleeping and always while I'm asleep that I'm going to die, and the more scared I am, the more pleasure and enlightenment I want to squeeze from every moment.' – Kenneth Tynan
10. 'A chapter of my life was closed and I felt a little nearer to inevitable death.' – Somerset Maugham (on leaving Tahiti)
11. 'When I look at the work of others I see only its merits; when I look at my own, I see only its faults.' – Claude Monet
12. 'Sleep after toyle, port after stormie seas, ease after warre, death after life does greatly please.' – Spenser (in Faerie Queene)

Freedom

Just as free speech and the freedom to think are under threat in schools and universities, so freedom is under threat in the world of medicine. In medicine the orthodoxy and the alternative are constantly at each other's throats and it is terribly difficult for patients to find the truth. Far too often, results are biased, hidden and fiddled to help further professional and commercial ambitions. Patients are left to suffer in a quagmire of confusion.

Journalism

George Orwell wrote that 'journalism is printing what someone else does not want printed; everything else is public relations'. Most national newspapers and magazines now print only press releases and opinions. Journalists no longer bother to hide their agendas.

Thoughts about Animals

1. 'Wild animals never kill for sport. Man is the only one to whom the torture and death of his fellow creatures is amusing in itself.' – James Anthony Froude
2. 'Until he extends the circle of his compassion to all living things, man will not himself find peace.' – Albert Schweizer
3. 'All animals are equal, but some animals are more equal than others.' – George Orwell
4. 'Nowadays we don't think much of a man's love for an animal; we mock people who are attached to cats. But if we stop loving animals, aren't we bound to stop loving humans too?' – Solzhenitsyn
5. 'A wild animal living free never poisons itself, for it knows what foods to choose. This is an instinct animals lose when they are domesticated.' – Maurice Messegue
6. 'Animals are such agreeable friends - they ask no questions, they pass no criticisms.' – George Elliot
7. 'There are two things for which animals are to be envied: they know nothing of future evils, or of what people say about them.' – Voltaire

8. 'Until one has loved an animal, a part of one's soul remains unawakened.' – Anatole France

9. 'When the kunkis (tame elephants) are sick, the mahouts take them to the forest where the elephants pick the herbs or plants they need. Somehow they're able to prescribe their own medicine.' – Dinesh Choudhury

10. 'Whosoever tortures animals has no soul, and the good spirit of the God is not in him. Even should he look deep inside himself, one can never trust him.' – Johann Wolfgang von Goethe

Old Age

'Old age is the stage of life that helps us grasp who we are, what we were for, and what our life has meant.' – *Jack King*

Liberty

'Liberty is the faculty of choosing the constraints one will accept.' – *Jean-Louis Barrault*

Freedom

'Freedom does not die in one blow, it dies by inches in public legislation.' – *Lord Strathclyde*

Horsewhipped

'I deserve to be horsewhipped.' – *Alan Clark, MP (After it was revealed that Mr Clark had bedded the wife of a judge and both of the couple's daughters).*

Hogs

'No man should be allowed to be President, who does not understand hogs.' – *Harry Truman*

Alain

In February 2024, gendarmes seized 72 guns and 3,000 rounds of ammunition from the home of French film star Alain Delon. Monsieur Delon, who died later the same year, did not have a gun licence.

Riots

When American students protested against the Vietnam War, the police foolishly arrested author Norman Mailer and threw him into the back of a police van (Mailer subsequently wrote 'Armies of the Night') and Dr Benjamin Spock, the author of multi-million selling 'Baby and Child Care'. These arrests helped change American history.

The authorities in Paris were much cleverer. During the student riots of 1968, Jean-Paul Sartre popped out of Deux Magots café to join in, and Sartre was duly arrested for civil disobedience. However, President Charles de Gaulle intervened and pardoned him saying: 'you don't arrest Voltaire'. (Actually, of course, Voltaire was arrested and imprisoned without trial in the Bastille.)

Vaccines

There have been numerous attempts to ban my book on vaccines and vaccination. I knew things had got out of hand when Joe Biden's White House tried to get the book banned – presumably because it was full of facts. I've been studying vaccines for most of my life and I would rather die or go to prison rather than allow myself to be injected with one of the toxic mRNA vaccines which are now so fashionable.

Crafty Nell
Nell Gwyn wasn't always a favourite with King Charles II. At one point she had a rival called Moll Davis. Fed up with seeing Moll being taken into the king's bedroom, Nell fed her a collection of cakes and sweetmeats which were packed with laxative herbs. The purgative effect produced something of an explosion in the King's bed that evening. As a contemporary writer put it 'the effects had such an operation upon the harlot when the king was caressing her in bed with the amorous sports of Venus that a violent and sudden looseness obliged her Ladyship to discharge her artillery. She put the king, as well as herself, in a most lamentable pickle which caused her royal master to turn her off with a small pension of a thousand pounds per annum in consideration of her former services in the affairs of love. After which she never appeared at court again.' And Nell was back in business.

The Pig
'There exists perhaps in all creation no animal which has less justice and more injustice shown than the pig.' – *Sir Frances Bond Head*

Socialism
'Socialism will triumph by capturing the culture via infiltration of schools, universities, churches and the media – transforming the consciousness of society.' – *Antonio Gramsci (founding member of the Communist Party of Italy)*

Best Western Movies

Shane
Rio Bravo
High Noon

Aggression
'Man is not made for peaceful intercourse with his fellows; he is by nature self-assertive, commonly aggressive, always critical in a more or less hostile spirit of any characteristic which seems alien to him…The average man or woman is always at open discord with someone; the great majority could not live without oft-recurrent squabbles.' – *George Gissing*

Life
'What is this life if, full of care, we have no time to stand and stare.' – *W.H.Davies*

Paranoia
'Only the paranoid survive.' – *Andy Grove*

Power
'Nothing in the world is more haughty than a man of moderate capacity when once raised to power.' – *Baron Wessenberg*

The Lame Kitten
'The fastest horse cannot catch a mouse as well as a lame kitten.' – *Chinese saying*

Electricity

Lots of things puzzle me. Here's one. There are, as everyone knows, two forms of electricity: direct current and alternating current. With direct current the electricity always travels in one direction. That I understand. It makes sense. But with alternating current the electricity constantly changes direction. First, it goes one way along the wire and then it turns round and goes the other way. I can't help wondering if this could possibly explain why every electrical appliance I own, or have ever owned, stops working from time to time. One minute it's working properly. And the next minute it's not. Maybe the thing (television or computer or whatever) stops working when the electricity turns round and goes backwards instead of going forwards. And could this explain why it is often possible to 'repair' an electrical item by turning it off and then back on again? Maybe when you do this you give yourself a chance of switching on just as the electricity is travelling in the right direction. You'd have a 50/50 chance of it going the right way, wouldn't you? I'm sure all the electrical engineers and boffins have thought of this. Or have they? Anyway, it's just one of many, many things that puzzles me.

Vegetarians

'If modern civilized man had to kill the animals he eats, the number of vegetarians would rise astronomically.' – *Christian Morgenstern*

Slaughter and Justice

'As long as people will shed the blood of innocent creatures there can be no peace, no liberty, no harmony between people. Slaughter and justice cannot dwell together.' – *Isaac Bashevis Singer*

Marginal Gains

Leading athletes are, apparently, all wearing the same brand of running shoe; a shoe which appears to have an advantage over all other shoes. Athletes who do not wear that brand are, of course, complaining that they don't stand a chance. It seems that the shoe which helps is lighter and designed rather differently. It has the usual cushioning but the mid sole is stiffened and this helps to reduce the amount of energy runners expend during a race. By reducing the energy they use up they can, of course, run faster.

The concept of 'marginal gains' is now extremely popular in all forms of athletics. I was impressed by the way the Sky cycling team used the technique to win the Tour de France several times but, of course, the idea of improving competitiveness by using the right equipment isn't a new one. I can still remember how French cyclist Laurent Fignon lost the Tour de France by eight seconds in 1989. The final stage of the Tour was a time trial, and the entirely unexpected winner was an American called Greg Lemond who was using special handlebars and an aerodynamic cycling helmet. Fignon rode with ordinary handlebars and no helmet.

The principle of marginal gains has been recognised for decades. A French director sportif called Cyrille Guimard, who looked after five times Tour de France winner Bernard Hinault, was a proponent of marginal gains. The people who originally devised this philosophy realised that the three week-long Tour de France is often won by a relatively small time gap and that the very top cyclists are pretty much of a muchness. There isn't that much difference between them. And most have the same basic training programme. It is therefore vital to do everything possible to gain small improvements. If you find a new type of material for cycling shorts which reduces air resistance and gives you a second a day then take that second a day. If you find that feeding the cyclists brown rice gives them another second a day then feed them brown rice. And so on and so on. The aim is that by making tiny improvements you will eventually end up with an advantage of a couple of minutes in a three week race. And that couple of minutes will be enough to win.

I firmly believe that this theory can be applied to medicine in general and, in particular, to tackling cancer. All this is of significance because the concept of 'marginal gains' is, of course, precisely what patients should do to keep themselves healthy and to improve their survival chances when they are ill. For example, there are many things that cancer patients can do to improve their chances. Some of the gains may be small but they are cumulative and 2% here and 3% there soon add up to an important number. If you find a treatment that adds a 20% improvement then you take it. If you find a treatment that adds a possible 3% improvement but has a probable 5% chance of making things worse then you don't take that one.

Enjoyment
'All animals except man know that the ultimate aim of life is to enjoy it.' – *Samuel Butler*

Epitaph
'Life is a jest, and all things show it;
I thought so once, and now I know it.' – *John Gay (a tombstone verse he wrote for himself)*

Lying
'We know they are lying. They know they are lying. They know that we know they are lying. We know that they know that we know they are lying. And still they continue to lie.' – *Solzhenitsyn*

Stuffing the Council
When Mr Richard Butler heard that the Derby City Council wanted to build a ring road through his garden, Mr Butler was rather cross but instead of chaining himself to a fence or climbing a tree he put up a banner protesting against the new road and giving the address of the website run by a protest group. The council responded by

prosecuting him for illegal advertising (claiming that the website address was a commercial logo). Mr Butler responded to that typically high handed snottiness by selling plots of his lawn to supporters for £1 a time. The council was then left with the job of tracking down all the co-owners of the lawn and serving them with individual compulsory purchase orders. This was made more difficult by the fact that the co-owners lived as far afield as Shanghai and Florence. The council leader responded by saying that he was very disappointed that Mr Butler had 'indulged in these delaying tactics'.

Old Age
'Old age is a time of leisure and freedom; freed from the factitious urgencies of earlier days, I am free to explore whatever I wish, and to bind the thoughts and feelings of a lifetime together.' – *Oliver Sachs*

Cannibalism in Scotland: The Strange Tale of Sawney Beane

You may not have heard of Sawney Beane. Some Scots (ashamed and embarrassed perhaps) like to pretend that he didn't exist. But he did. He was as real as haggis and Robert Burns. He was born in East Lothian, Scotland during the reign of Queen Elizabeth (the first one, not the second one) and when he found the family trade of hedging and ditching to be too much like hard work, he found a wife and set off to find a less strenuous life. The young couple chose to live in a cave on the rocky coast of Galloway. The cave was deep and required no expenditure, though the front of it filled with water at high tide.

Neither Mr nor Mrs Beane were keen on hard work and not terribly enthusiastic about growing food or hunting for it. They quickly realised that humans were the type of quarry easiest to catch. There were plenty of travellers on the nearby highway and the people wandering by, on horseback or on foot, weren't usually armed or prepared to defend themselves. Moreover, humans wore clothing which could be appropriated and recycled.

The Beanes started in quite a small way. They clubbed to death solitary travellers and the consumable pieces they didn't eat raw they pickled and stored to provide for rainy days.

But as the Beane family grew, so they found that the odd traveller didn't satisfy all their requirements and they started to travel further afield into the countryside. Soon the number of unexplained disappearances grew and became something of a talking point in the region. When individuals or families disappeared, suspicions fell on strangers who were frequently arrested on suspicion of murder. Local innkeepers were arrested and executed too and eventually most of the local hostelries closed. The authorities tried to find out what was going on but got nowhere. Indeed, some of those looking for answers did not return from their investigations.

As the Beane children grew so they were recruited to the family business. The young Beanes didn't meet outsiders without killing and eating them and so they bred exclusively among themselves.

The Beanes may have been psychopaths but they were not entirely stupid. They kept the entrance to their cave free of litter (bones and such like) and tried to ensure that there were no witnesses to their killing.

Things went well for the Beanes and they had been eating people for thirty years when disaster struck.

The Beanes attacked a man and his wife who were riding a horse back from a fair. They pulled the woman from the horse and cut her throat. However, the husband wasn't so easy to kill and while the girls of the family drank the woman's blood, he used his sword and pistol to attack the rest of the Beane family. He was so successful in this that he was still alive when a group of twenty travellers from the fair appeared, saw what was happening and joined in. The Beanes, not accustomed to defending themselves, fled the scene.

There were now witnesses to what was going on in the area.

The Provost of Glasgow was informed and he passed on the news to King James (who was the Scottish monarch at the time) and the king, accompanied by four hundred soldiers and a pack of bloodhounds hurried into the area.

Eventually, the bloodhounds found the Beane's cave and all the members of the family were arrested. There were by then the original two Beanes plus eight sons, six daughters, eighteen grandsons and fourteen granddaughters. The ceiling of the cave was decorated with a larder of dangling limbs and the corners of the cave were full of stolen clothing, weapons and jewellery.

It wasn't considered necessary to waste public money on a trial.

Sawney Beane and his large family were taken first to Edinburgh and then to Leith. Sawney, his sons and grandsons all had their hands and feet chopped off and Mrs Beane, the daughters and granddaughters were placed on a pyre and burned to death. They all cursed a good deal but not one of them repented.

And that is the true and astonishing story of Sawney Beane and his family.

Witness
Here is a list of seven things I would have liked to have witnessed.
1) Jesus throwing the money lenders out of the temple
2) Jesus Christ giving the sermon on the mount
3) Moses parting the Red Sea
4) Cromwell dissolving Parliament
5) Elizabeth 1st's speech at Tilbury
6) Churchill being saved by Lawrence of Arabia when threatened by a crowd of angry Arabs
7) Napoleon returning from Elba and turning the army behind him

Chemotherapy
The word 'chemotherapy' is much misunderstood. It has been hijacked to mean the treatment of disease (usually cancer) with a cytotoxic substance (something that kills cells). But the word really means the treatment of a disease with a chemical substance. If you take aspirin for a headache or an antibiotic for an infection you are undergoing chemotherapy. This definition may sometimes be used in rather disingenuous ways.

Extraordinary students

These days, students can be thrown out of university for making a thoughtless comment on social media or appearing in an inappropriate video on the internet. It wasn't always this way. Beau Nash, who styled himself the King of Bath, and was a student at Jesus College, Oxford, got away without censorship even though he rode naked through an Oxfordshire village. He was sitting on a cow at the time. Lord Byron attended Trinity College, Cambridge and responded to the college's 'no dogs' rule by arriving with a pet bear in tow. The 2nd Earl of Rochester began his studies at Wadham College, Oxford at the age of 13 and quickly became notorious and debauched. He left with an MA a year later. Mad Jack Mytton arrived at Cambridge University in 1816 with 2,000 bottles of port to sustain him. But he got bored and left. Still, students did sometimes get into trouble in days gone by. In 1883, the Royal College of Physicians and Surgeons at Queen's University in Kingston, Canada, expelled all female students. Their crime? They weren't male.

Crooks

In no area of life are there as many convicted criminals as there are in politics.

Security

Never use your real birthday on the internet. And never give your real phone number. I pick a date at random for my birthday. The phone number I give used to be the phone number of the head office of the company demanding that I give it. When this became boring and a little tedious (because companies often keep their phone number secret these days) I bought a very cheap burner phone, threw it away and kept the phone number to use whenever I am required to give a number.

Long term
Try to think long term. York Minster took 245 years to build and many generations worked on the building. They took great pride in their craftsmanship.

Bosom bottle
In the 19th century women used to wear flowers in their cleavage; the flowers were usually held in place within a bosom bottle, a silver cone covered with ribbon, which was lodged between the breasts; the bosom bottle sometimes contained a little water to keep the flowers looking fresh.

Wyatt Earp
Wyatt Berry Stapp Earp of Dodge City, Tombstone and the OK Corral, refereed the world heavyweight boxing championship match between Bob Fitzsimmons and Tom Sharkey in 1896. Not a lot of people know that.

Campaigning
After more than half a century of campaigning for people and animals, I can assure you that if you become involved in any sort of campaign then your main enemies will not be the people you think of as the opposition but will be some of the people who appear to be on your side. I am afraid that the two most potent and destructive driving forces in any campaign are greed and jealousy. Too many of those who become involved in campaigning are more interested in protecting the bit of turf they have marked out for themselves than actually achieving anything. It is for this reason that attempts to combine different groups with the same general aim will always fail.

Things I have Learned
1. If you have to think too hard about what is right and what is wrong then you're in real danger of doing the wrong thing.
2. Ignore the future and remember from the past only that which is encouraging and which warms your heart.
3. Do not allow others to make decisions for you. Make your own decisions. And treat others with respect not subservience. If you make the wrong choice then at least it was your choice.
4. At whatever age you are, life without a purpose is purposeless. Without meaning, a life is stagnant.
5. People have become incredibly good at wasting time. Be aware that huge industries have developed which are designed to do nothing else but make time-wasting ever easier.
6. Rich food and drink are just some of the delights which the elderly must eschew. Other lost delights include climbing trees, running up hills and something which I cannot now remember.
7. Remember that in life it is always the journey rather than the destination that matters.

The Sizzle
The phrases 'Don't sell the steak – sell the sizzle' and 'Turn your lemons into lemonade' were both invented by super-salesman Elmer Wheeler.

Audiences
Cinema audiences never really warmed to Alec Guinness. They admired him as an actor but they never loved him. But they loved Peter O'Toole. Many thespians could never understand this, but the explanation is a simple one: Guinness played characters with both feet firmly on the ground, whereas O'Toole's characters, full of drama and excitement, were never real. Cinema goers don't really go to the cinema to see 'real'. They can see 'real' if they peer over the

garden fence.

The Last Day

'Live each day as if it were your last' is a dangerous maxim. What would I do if I knew, without doubt, that I would be dead by midnight? I really don't think you want to know. And since I'd be arrested for the thought, I don't think I want the authorities to know. Antoinette's version of this maxim is much better: 'Live every day as if it is your birthday.'

Voting

Whenever I am sent a voting form (for a company, charity or club) I consider it my duty to vote against everything promoted or favoured by the board of directors or managing committee. Most people vote as they are told to vote. A few 'no' votes can help keep committees and boards of directors a little more honest. And in political elections I vote for independent candidates rather than the candidates who represent political parties. The independent candidates are usually the most honest ones.

Joy

Happiness can occasionally be bought.

When Antoinette came out of a pharmacy recently she headed for the car and was suddenly stopped by an elderly man who was smiling broadly. He shook her hand and the two of them then hugged.

When she got back into the car, Antoinette explained that when she had been in the pharmacy she had heard the old man and his wife asking the assistant about the cost of hot water bottles. The assistant told the couple that they had two hot water bottles in stock, a red one and a blue one, and that they cost £4.99 each. She put the hot water bottles on the counter for them to examine. The couple then counted their money and, after some discussion, realised that they didn't have enough cash to purchase the two hot water bottles. They didn't want to buy just one because they wanted one each.

Antoinette picked up the two hot water bottles. 'I'll take these please,' she said to the assistant. And when she had paid for them she turned and handed the two hot water bottles to the old couple who, although heading for the door to leave the shop, had turned and were looking on, rather surprised to see 'their' hot water bottles being bought so quickly by another customer.

'These are a present,' said Antoinette.

A random act of kindness.

And that is why the old man hugged Antoinette when she came out of the shop.

Adolf Beck

Born in Norway in 1844, Adolf Beck came to England in 1885. He worked as a mining engineer but not very successfully. On 16th December 1895, in London, he was confronted by a woman who accused him of stealing two rings and a watch from her. He tried to ignore her but she persisted. Beck complained to a policeman that she was a prostitute who was bothering him. The woman, Miss Ottilie Meissonier, insisted Beck was a thief. The policeman took the pair to the police station where Beck was arrested. In due course, 22 other women claimed that they had been robbed by Beck. Their stories were identical. Each had been approached by a man calling himself Lord Wilton de Willoughby and on each occasion the fake peer had pretended to mistake the woman for a fake Lady Everton. Wilton de Willoughby was immensely charming and boasted to the women about his estate and yacht. He flattered them and invited them to sail with him on the Riviera. He gave each a cheque to buy suitable clothes for the South of France and asked to borrow their rings and other jewellery so that he could match the sizes and find better ones. Amazingly, 23 women fell for this extraordinary story and all were disappointed, shocked and astonished when their cheques bounced. They later all picked out Beck at an identification parade, though this was hardly a fair exercise since Beck was the only grey haired man with a moustache in the line-up.

This extraordinary but successful scam had previously been used by a man calling himself John Smith who had been imprisoned in 1877, and the policeman who had arrested Beck swore on the bible that Lord Wilton de Willoughby was John Smith (or vice versa). Beck's lawyers argued that this was nonsense because their client had been in South America in 1877 when Smith had been in court. It was also proved that whereas Smith had been Jewish, Beck was not Jewish.

The trial of the unfortunate Beck was a farce. The judge, Sir Forrest Fulton, had been the prosecutor in the John Smith trial and he appeared to have bent over backwards to put Beck in prison. Inevitably, Beck went down for seven years.

Beck was released in 1901 and although poor, he survived well enough until 1904 when a woman called Pauline Scott reported that she had been scammed in the now traditional style. ('Let me take you to my yacht and buy you better rings.').

A police inspector took Ms Scott to confront Beck in the street. And Beck, by now understandably wary, tried to run. The inspector took this as a sign of guilt, caught him and arrested him. Almost immediately five more women turned up with similar stories. Apparently unembarrassed by their susceptibility to flattery and bribes, they all wrongly identified Beck as the trickster and the jury duly found him guilty once more.

Fortunately for Beck the judge, didn't believe the witnesses, wasn't convinced that Beck really was guilty and delayed sentencing.

And then, while Beck was locked up, another man was arrested for a similar scam. ('Let me take you to my yacht and buy you better rings.') This man called himself William Thomas but the police were convinced he was really John Smith.

And when women from both of Beck's trials were taken to see Thomas they all identified him as the man they had known as Smith. (His real name was, you will not be surprised to hear, neither Smith nor Thomas but Wilhelm Meyer, and he was Austrian.)

Smith/Thomas/Meyer admitted that he was responsible for all the thefts.

And so, in July 1904, Beck was duly pardoned and given compensation of £5,000 (worth the best part of half a million in today's money). Sir Forrest Fulton, the judge from Beck's first trial, was severely censured (though he should have been made to pay the compensation out of his own pocket) and the police were given a firm talking to because they knew (or should have known) that Beck wasn't Smith. As a result of this extraordinary farrago, the Court of Criminal Appeal was founded and Beck became so famous that at least one postcard company sold pictures of him to the public. Despite, or because of, his notoriety the hapless Beck died a sad and broken man – by no means the first or the last innocent man to be destroyed by the legal system.

Symmetry

I spent ten years working as a GP, ten years writing a column for the *Daily Star*, ten years writing a column for *The Sun* and ten years writing a column for *The People*. I find such inexplicable symmetry slightly disturbing.

Average Income

The idea of an average income is ludicrous and meaningless. If a road sweeper earns £19,000 a year and a hedge fund manager earns £1,981,000 a year their average income is £1,000,000 a year. The average income in a company, charity or government department will be heavily influenced by the boss's income which may be many times the average income of most of the workers.

Wonder Cures

Never allow yourself to be suckered by media stories into believing that a new wonder cure for (insert name of disease here) is just around the corner. For years now the mainstream media has been full of stories about new wonder drugs and treatments. These stories are fed to the press by scientists seeking grants or publicity, and I'm afraid that 99 out of 100 of these miracles never come to fruition.

Brooding
'Homo animal querulum cupide suis incumbens miseriis'. (A rough translation is: Man is a querulous animal – always loving to brood over his miseries). – *From 'The Private Papers of Henry Ryecroft' by George Gissing*

Stupidity
Never underestimate how stupid the young can be. A young Amazon delivery driver rang our door bell. I was at the far end of the house and even when I'm in a hurry I don't do much running these days (I know a woman who was rushing in her home and who tripped and spent six months having extensive facio-maxillary surgery to repair the face she battered when she fell forwards) and when I eventually opened the door, he handed me a letter sized package. 'You could have popped it through the letter box,' I told him. 'It would have saved you waiting.' He looked at me in genuine amazement. 'No one told me I could do that,' he said.

Life sentence
Antoinette met and spoke to a couple with a 25-year-old daughter in a wheelchair. They told her an awful story.

When the girl was a baby she was perfectly normal but she was hit on the head by her sister's boyfriend. The boyfriend was given three years in prison and was duly released to enjoy the rest of his life. The young girl and her family were, however, given a lifetime sentence. In addition to being brain damaged, the girl is blind.

Ageing

Ageing is becoming an emerging worry for young people who used to regard the elderly as inhabitants of another, far-off country but who now see the penniless, bleak future which awaits them, as they struggle to stay alive invisible, uncared for, unwanted, dependent and lonely in a world without compassion or health care.

Bottom Patting Machine

In January 1971, Thomas V Zelenka invented a machine designed to pat the bottom of a restless body. A rotary motor fitted to the side of a cot or crib is converted into back and forth motion and a soft mitten repeatedly pats the baby's bottom. The machine was given US Patent number 3,552,388. In 1989, Rita A. Delia Vecchia invented a scratching and petting device for pets which was awarded US Patent number 4,872,422. This device consists of a horizontal arm which can be raised or lowered according to the size of the pet and which swings from side to side. I have no idea whether either of these items were ever manufactured or sold but neither seems available on Amazon at the moment.

Houses

Modern houses are, like the paper houses which the Japanese used to favour, not built to last more than 20 or 30 years. Taking a fifty year mortgage on a house that won't last half that long is reckless; encouraging young couples to borrow money to buy modern houses is wicked.

Biopsies

When I was a junior doctor working as a house surgeon the surgeon would, if operating on a woman with suspected breast cancer, take a biopsy and send the sample to the lab to be examined. Before being anaesthetised, the patient would have signed two forms – one for a biopsy and one for whatever more serious operation might be needed. (In those days most cases of breast cancer resulted in a mastectomy). The surgeon, I and the nursing staff would then stand around and wait twenty minutes for the result. Twenty minutes. That's how long it took to obtain a biopsy result. Today, patients are often made to wait six weeks to get the result of a biopsy. That is scandalous. Everyone who has a biopsy should have the result back the same day.

Harry
I hope I'm around to read the books Prince Harry's kids write about their parents.

On the Run
A newspaper headline which read 'Octagenarians of Oz on the run' caught my eye in 2006. The story (a single column three inch squib) ran thus: 'An elderly couple went on the run in Australia for two weeks to avoid health authorities who they believed wanted to place them into care. British expatriates Mr and Mrs Foulkes hit the road in a battered Ford Mondeo in a bid to keep their freedom. Mr Foulkes, 81, who suffers from mild dementia and his 87-year-old wife who has Alzheimer's disease, vanished from their Melbourne home and travelled hundreds of miles across the country. They were recognised in Canberra as they checked into a hotel and later taken to a hospital. It is hoped they will eventually be able to return home with social worker support.' I used this rather thin but incredibly moving news story as the basis for my novel *Mr Henry Mulligan*. The tiny news stories often contain more real-life drama than the big ones.

Spies
The Secret Intelligence Services in the UK like to pretend that their history is exciting and their origins hidden amongst great mysteries.

The civil servants who are responsible for catching spies in the UK, and who are theoretically responsible for the nation's security, are known as MI5. The civil servants who are responsible for doing the spying (and who are supposed to work outside the UK) are known as MI6 (though they like to refer to themselves as 'the firm' or 'the friends' because this gives them an air of being something rather mysterious and special). The two groups got their names in a very mundane way. When Military Intelligence was first created, the individuals dealing with catching spies worked in a room with the number 5 on the door. Next to it, along the corridor, were the people responsible for doing the spying. They were in a room with the number 6 on the door. Hence MI5 and MI6. The eavesdropping for both services is done by a bunch of nosey parkers working in a huge and expensive building near Cheltenham Race Course which is known as the Government Communications Headquarters (known as GCHQ). The people working there spend their days listening to other people's phone calls and reading emails that the people who sent them thought were private. When the spies want to arrest someone, they need a policeman and so they call in Special Branch which was originally formed as part of London's Metropolitan Police.

Moving
The best film about moving into a new home is 'Mr Blandings Builds his Dream House' starring Cary Grant and Myrna Loy. Everyone planning to move house should watch it.

Happiness
'Above me and to my right shone the lights of the honest bungalow dwellers of Silverdale: I found myself envying them bitterly. It is chaps like them who have the secret of happiness, they know the art of it, they always knew it. Happiness is an annuity, or its shares in a Building Society; it's a pension and blue hydrangeas, and wonderfully clever grandchildren, and being on the Committee, and

just-a-few-earlies in the vegetable garden, and being alive and wonderful-for-his-age when old so-and-so is under the sod.' – *From 'Don't Point That Thing at Me' by Kyril Bonfiglioli*

The Stegosaurus
'It was, I think, the stegosaurus which had one brain in its head and another in its arse to control the tail…they managed to rule the world for about 140 million years, which sets a bench mark for any civil service.' – *Gavin Lyall*

Bone head
After Antoinette had been treated with radiotherapy for the best part of a month, she went to visit her unpleasant and rather useless GP complaining that she had developed neuropathy. 'Oh, I'm thinking bone cancer,' said the thoughtless GP immediately.

Surprise
I find it surprising that Jamaica and Trinidad (both in the West Indies) are about the same distance apart as are Malta and the Channel Islands.

Stomach
'You must laugh and be cheerful ten times a day or your stomach, that father of affliction, will disturb you in the night.' – *Frederick Nietzsche*

Knowing

'To know that you do not know is the best. To pretend to know when you do not is a disease.' – *Lao Tzu*

Drug interactions

Most (by which I mean nearly all) doctors seem woefully unaware of the fact that prescribed drugs don't always get on with one another. Doctors will happily prescribe a drug for a patient already taking another drug without bothering to check whether the two drugs are incompatible. I don't know whether they do this through ignorance or stupidity but it is a major cause of serious illness.

Pope Innocent III

In 1210, Pope Innocent III said that if men quarrelled over a game of chess and one of the players killed his opponent then the killer should not be charged with homicide.

They know you're fast, Clint.

Clint Eastwood and a film director were discussing a scene in a film in which Eastwood was expected to shoot one of the bad guys. And he was supposed to do so effortlessly and quickly. Eastwood asked the director if they shouldn't include a scene to establish that his character was fast with a gun. The director said that this wasn't necessary. 'They know you're fast, Clint,' he responded.

When making movies with big stars, directors always have to remember the star's film reputation. Alfred Hitchcock knew better than to cast Cary Grant as a crook or a murderer. Before they sat down to watch a movie the audience knew that Cary Grant was the good guy and would get the girl. Joseph Cotton could play a murderer but Cary Grant couldn't.' John Wayne was often gruff and bad-tempered but invariably a good guy at heart; decent and honourable. Dean Martin was always a drinker.

And Clint Eastwood was always quick with a gun.

The irony is that in reality, Eastwood was not, apparently, all that quick a draw. When Eastwood and the magnificent Lee van Cleef were making the classic film 'A Few Dollars More', the crew organised a quick draw contest between the two. And Lee van Cleef won the competition.

Film buffs who have studied movies frame by frame reckon, however, that Lee van Cleef wasn't the fastest of them all. That honour apparently (and rather surprisingly) goes to Glenn Ford.

I don't think big John Wayne came anywhere on the list. But then his characters often used a rifle rather than a handgun.

Experiments

There is no law in the United Kingdom law which states that drug and cosmetic companies have to test their products on animals. Companies do their testing on animals so that they can use good results to promote their products but can ignore bad results by claiming that animals are different to people.

Vincent

In the 1920s there was a cottage industry in diagnosing Vincent Van Gogh. The official diagnoses offered included:
Acute mania with general delirium
Meningo encephalitis
Epileptic hallucinations
Solar intoxication
Paralysis after syphilis
Oedipus complex
Narcissism
Homosexuality
Alcoholic epilepsy
If I had to throw my guess into the ring I'd say he was a manic depressive (and would today be diagnosed as having bipolar disease) with an overlay of paranoia, a touch of schizophrenia and a dose of mixed neuroses all grossly exacerbated by his frequent use of

absinthe. But your guess is as good as mine and as good as anyone else's. Who cares now? He may have suffered disappointments and frustrations in life but in death he has given great joy to untold millions.

Robert Wilson

The kindest, gentlest journalist I ever met was called Robert Hendrie Wilson. When I met him he was Features Editor on the *Sunday Mirror* in London. Like many people who worked in Fleet Street in the latter part of the 20th century, Robert had a well-developed affection for alcohol and tobacco. I don't think I ever saw him without a cigarette between browned fingers, and he was the first person I met who actually had bottles of booze in his filing cabinet. The first time he came to visit me in Devon he prepared himself for the two hour train journey by buying two large bottles of gin and 200 cigarettes (one of the packs usually sold in airport shops). He was, he said, worried that the buffet might not be open or that their supplies might prove inadequate for the journey.

A Short Prayer

I discovered a short prayer: 'Thank you for everything just as it is.'

At first I was dismissive. Why would we want things as they are? And then I realised how much worse they could be.

It's actually what most of us want, isn't it – for things to stay the same.

But they never do stay the same. Not for long anyway.

Of course, when people want things to change, that's when they are likely to stay the same.

After I had thanked God for everything just as it is, I asked Him to please leave it that way.

Theft

There are many different kinds of theft. My wife is a professional artist. She sells original paintings and prints, and used to sell greeting cards of her work. She stopped allowing shops to sell greeting cards when a man boasted that he had saved himself some money by buying one of her greetings cards and having it enlarged to the size of a print so that he could frame it and hang it over his fireplace. It wasn't the loss of the sale that irked her as much as the man's sheer delight in having cheated her.

The Poor
'There is a virulent section of left wingers who don't want to help the poor; they just want to punish those who aren't poor' – *Flavio Cipollini*

General Practice in the UK
After being diagnosed with breast cancer, Antoinette telephoned our GP's surgery to make an appointment. To my astonishment (and horror) Antoinette was told that she couldn't have an appointment to see her GP for three weeks or more. Antoinette explained that she had just been diagnosed with breast cancer and that for much of August she would be at the hospital every day for radiotherapy. The receptionist was adamant. The best she could do was to arrange for the GP to telephone her the following week.

On another occasion, not long after her diagnosis, Antoinette had a call from the GPs' surgery. A receptionist told Antoinette that one of the GPs wanted to speak to her on the telephone. She was told that an appointment has been made for the GP to ring her in eight days' time. She was told that her GP, who has received a letter from the hospital, would ring her then and tell her something, possibly to her disadvantage. We had no idea what the call would be about or what the something might be. We were so accustomed to waiting for news that eight days seemed a perfectly reasonable period of time to wait to receive a telephone call.

I like to think that I am a gentle, forgiving sort of person but if I had my way these people would be boiled in oil, hung drawn and quartered, dragged through the streets, beheaded and burnt alive. Is that unreasonable?

Autry

I doubt if many people remember Gene Autry. The few who do, probably know him only as 'the singing cowboy'. But Autry was much, much more than a successful star of over 50 westerns. Songs he made famous include 'Frosty the Snowman', 'Rudolph the Red Nosed Reindeer', 'You are my sunshine', 'Blueberry Hill' and 'Home on the Range'. He wrote many popular songs which are still regularly recorded and performed – including the evergreen 'Here comes Santa Claus'. He had a long running hit radio show (Gene Autry's Melody Ranch) and when television began he started a (long running) TV show (The Gene Autry Show). His horse Champion had his own radio show. When he died (aged 91 in 1998) Autry was worth an estimated $320 million. His estate must still be earning millions.

Flyer

Antoine de Saint-Exupery, the French author and aviator, wrote several wonderful books about flying (the best of which is *Wind Sand and Stars*) but is most famous for having written *The Little Prince* (published posthumously in France) which has been translated into 250 languages and is one of the top selling books in the world, though, of course, Saint-Exupery never knew any of this. On July 31st 1944, Saint-Exupery, then 44-years-old, took off from the Island of Corsica flying a Lockheed Lightning P38 reconnaissance plane. His task was to collect intelligence on German troop movements in and around the Rhone Valley. He never returned and his disappearance remained a mystery for years. There were theories that he had lost control of his aeroplane or that he had deliberately committed suicide by flying into the sea. (Saint-Exupery had been wrongly said to have been a supporter of the Vichy Regime in France and as a result of the libel, he had become depressed and was drinking heavily.) In 1998, divers finally found the damaged remains of his plane after a fisherman found a bracelet with Saint-Exupery's name engraved on it. Further lengthy investigations suggested that the plane had been shot down by a German pilot called Horst Rippert. 'I shot down Saint-Exupery,' said Rippert in 2008. The ultimate, tragic irony is that Rippert had read a number of Saint-Exupery's books and was a huge fan. 'If I had known what I was doing I would never have done it,' he is reported to have said, riddled with shame and guilt at having killed his hero. There is a small bust of Saint-Exupery in a tiny park near to Les Invalides in Paris.

Origins

'Consider your origin. You were not formed to live like brutes but to follow virtue and knowledge.' – *Dante Alighieri*

Perk

I've never really had any perks because I've never really had a job. But when I was a medical student, the Queen Elizabeth Hospital in Birmingham used to allow staff (and students) to eat free in the canteen after midnight. Impoverished students ate most of their hot meals after midnight. That was a perk worth having and provided a welcome change from pie and chips (we couldn't afford fish) or Chinese takeaway meals.

Advice

Here are three pieces of advice which all GPs would do well to remember. First, when a mother says that her child is ill then the child is almost certainly ill. Mothers know best and often know better than doctors. Indeed, this is pretty well true for patients of all ages. I made it a rule always to visit patients at home, whatever time of day or night, if they or a relative wanted to see a doctor. If I talked to a patient on the telephone I would always end the consultation by asking if they wanted me to visit. Most of the time they said no, it wasn't necessary. And I always told them that if things changed, or they were worried, they should ring back. Next, doctors should visit frail and elderly patients at home once every two weeks. These days, of course, the vast majority of doctors never see patients in their own homes. Doctors who do not visit their patients at home are failing themselves and their patients.

Book Sales

Excluding The Bible (which is estimated to have sold five billion copies), the Qur'an, the Book of Mormon and other religious books, the top selling books in the world (the top seven of which have each sold over 100 million copies) are:

A Tale of Two Cities – Charles Dickens
The Little Prince – Antoine de Saint-Exupery
The Alchemist – Paulo Coelho
Harry Potter and the Philosopher's Stone – J.K.Rowling
And Then There Were None – Agatha Christie
Dream of the Red Chamber – Cao Xueqin
The Hobbit – J.R.R.Tolkein
She: A History of Adventure – H.Rider Haggard
The Da Vinci Code – Dan Brown
The Catcher in the Rye – J.D.Salinger

The biggest selling non-fiction book which isn't a religious volume has for many years been 'The Common Sense Book of Baby and Child Care' by Benjamin Spock, which is estimated to have sold 50 million copies worldwide since its first publication in 1946.

Missing Stamps

In 1855, a delivery of 55,000 stamps were due to arrive in British Guiana, a British colony in South America. The stamps had been sent from Britain but unfortunately, 50,000 of the stamps failed to arrive on time. (No one knows what happened to them and it's probably too late to expect them to turn up now, though no doubt there is someone still waiting in hope.) This shortage gave the local postmaster a headache. Without stamps the colony's letters and newspapers could not be delivered. So the postmaster arranged for the local newspaper to print some one cent stamps (for use on newspapers) and four cent stamps (for letters). The home-made stamps carried an illustration of a ship and the British Guiana motto 'We give and we ask in return'. These weren't supposed to be real stamps but were produced to keep things moving while waiting for the official stamps to turn up. And when a replacement consignment of 50,000 stamps eventually arrived in British Guiana, the local postmaster destroyed the ersatz and entirely unofficial stamps and thought no more about them. Since stamp collecting didn't exist as a hobby none of the ersatz stamps were kept. Except one. Eighteen years after it was thought that the home-made stamps had all been destroyed and forgotten, a 12-year-old school boy called Vernon Vaughan found a one cent stamp (coloured Magenta) while rummaging around among some of his uncle's papers. (I like to think that he was rummaging with permission.) He sold the stamp for six shillings which doesn't sound much now but was a fortune in 1873, especially for a 12-year-old boy who probably thought Christmas had come early. Six shillings in 1873 would be the equivalent of around £40-£50 today. Of course, if he'd kept the stamp in good condition and had lived to be 150-years-old he'd now be a multi-millionaire. There is no record of who bought the stamp from young Master Vaughan but it next ended up in the collection of a collector in Liverpool called Philipp von Ferrary. When Mr Ferrary died in 1917 the stamp was sold for $32,500 to an American called Arthur Hind. (You do not, you see, have to be Prime Minister or write a great novel in order to achieve immortality. All you need to do is to buy, and possess for a while, an exceedingly rare stamp.) The stamp was inevitably sold and resold a number of times and each time it was sold the price paid seemed to soar way past inflation. By 1980, the stamp was sold for $935,000 and in 2014 a show designer called Stuart Weitzman bought the stamp in New York for $9,500,000. Unfortunately, Mr Weitzman doesn't seem to have made a profit on the world's rarest and most valuable stamp for when he sold it in 2021 it was bought for $8.3 million by the British stamp dealing company Stanley Gibbons.

Blitzkrieg
In 1840, the Germans invented a new form of warfare which they called Blitzkrieg – it involved very fast, furious attacks from all directions. These days it sometimes seems that our governments are using the same form of warfare in their attacks on us.

Too nice
If you treat people too nicely some will see you as weak, will take you for granted and will exploit you.

Weapons
The best weapons are unpredictability and letting the enemy know that you are fighting on a matter of principle – and have nothing to lose

Embarrassment
A young female university student was embarrassed that her father was a postman. She described him to her college friends as a man of letters.

The 400
A journalist Ward McAllister said in the late 19th century that there were only about four hundred acceptable people in fashionable New York society. 'If you go outside that number you strike people who are either not at ease in a ballroom or else make other people not at

ease.'

McAllister eventually produced a list of the 400 – those who had been invited to Mrs Caroline Astor's ball in 1892. The list was entirely his making but continued to exist for generations.

Belle of the Ball

Every young belle in 19th century New York was expected to have 45 gowns, seven cloaks, 48 chemises, nine fans, seven jewelled combs, twenty hair nets, a set of Russian sables (cape, muff and boa) together with a selection of card cases and gold whist markers.

Tossed in a blanket

The richest man in America, John Jacob Astor died in 1848 after a long illness. In his last years his servants regularly tossed him gently in a blanket to stir his sluggish blood. The only food Astor could digest was milk from the breast of a wet nurse.

Freedom

We should be free to be wrong, even to appear ridiculous, as long as our thoughts and beliefs do not cause physical or mental harm to those around us. But we are not free. Original thought, thinking that outrages or even upsets the establishment, is suppressed, oppressed and punished with a vehemence which would have elicited notes of approval from Torquemada, Mussolini and Stalin. I can assure you, from personal experience, that modern truth tellers are punished for daring to share unacceptable truths.

The Library with no Books

A town council in England built a brand new public library and equipped it with all the latest computers and software. There were miles of elegant shelving. It was only at the official opening, attended by the usual local dignitaries and a couple of local authors for extra spice, that anyone noticed that there were no books in the library. And since all the available money had been spent on building the library there were no funds left to buy books. The library remained empty.

Rejects

Irving Stone's book about Vincent van Gogh (*Lust for Life*) was rejected by just about every publisher in existence. But Stone's book became one of the world's biggest selling novels and helped boost the public's interest in van Gogh. Twenty two years after publication, the book was adapted into a film starring Kirk Douglas. Two of my own most successful books (*Bodypower* and *Alice's Diary*) were rejected by just about every publisher in London. Both are still in print, and selling well, decades after they were eventually published.

Elderly

The elderly become irritated and grumpy when they see the young making the same mistakes as they themselves made half a century earlier. And the grumpiness is exacerbated when the young steadfastly refuse to listen to advice built on painful experiences.

Empty

'There is, quite possibly, nowhere quite as good for quiet contemplation and reflection as an empty sports ground.' – T.Robinson who want us all to stop using fossil fuels suggest that sunshine is inexhaustible. They are wrong. We are already using as much sunshine as we can. Plants cannot be grown in deserts or at the poles, and crop production depends upon rainfall and temperature as well as sunshine. Since 1986, it has been known that there is a photosynthetic ceiling. At that time it was estimated that we were already using at least half of the available sunshine and that much of the rest was being wasted because it was falling on roads and built up areas. Areas of land covered with solar panels do turn sunshine into electricity for industrial and domestic purposes but the land so covered is lost to farming and so they do more harm than good.' – *Jack King*

Truth

It was Schopenhauer who said that 'all truth passes through three stages. First it is ridiculed. Second, it is violently opposed. Third, it is accepted as self-evident.' This is absolutely true of all attempts to introduce fresh, original thinking into any aspect of human life, including medical practice.

Competition

When I worked as a columnist for *The People* newspaper, the circulation was around three million. One Sunday, the paper organised a competition for the readers. Numbers were printed in the paper. The winner would be the one with the winning numbers printed in their copy of the paper. Unfortunately, something went wrong and around three million readers all won the £1,000,000 first prize. Staff in the competitions department spent a good many hours trying to explain the error to readers who had telephoned to claim their prize and who were disappointed to learn that they had not become millionaires. If the paper had been forced to pay all the winners the cost would have exceeded the number of noughts which my calculator can manage.

Balance
Young people don't want to work and they talk incessantly about work-life balance as though it were something they had just discovered, but what precisely are they planning to do with their lives? Work gives satisfaction, as well as helping the worker to earn a living, pay their own way, be independent and help others.

Dressing
'All women dress like their mothers. That is their tragedy. No man does. That is his.' – *Alan Bennett*

Radium
There have been as many fashions in medicine as in women's clothing. So, for example, going back in history there are many examples of 'cures' based on radium being offered to a gently believing (and often desperate) public. Worst of the lot was William Aloysius Bailey, an American who pretended to be a doctor and marketed a variety of products based on radium. His most profitable product was 'Certified Radioactive Water'. One patient drank 1,500 bottles of it (on the recommendation of a real doctor) and died of radiation poisoning. That was well over half a century ago and his bones are reported to be still highly radioactive. In the 1930s there were heaps of products sold with radium in them – including soap, chocolate, contraceptives, cigarettes, toothpaste and beauty creams. You could buy bourbon aged with radium. There was even a cookbook for chefs who wanted to bake with radium. *The American Journal of Clinical Care* claimed that 'radioactivity prevents insanity, rouses noble emotions, retards old age and creates a splendid, youthful, joyous life'.

Thoreau

David Henry Thoreau said that we should consider things in terms of the time we spent in acquiring them. How many hours of your life did you have to give in order to acquire that ornament or that new pair of shoes. And William Morris, of course, said that we should all have nothing in our homes that is not beautiful or useful.

Gamesmanship

From 1993 onwards I wrote the agony column for a Sunday newspaper called *The People*. Towards the end of the millennium I had lunch with the editor and deputy editor to discuss my contract.

'How much do you want?' asked the editor, as we approached the end of our meal.

I thought for a moment. 'A hundred thousand plus a 12% a year,' I said.

I've always preferred my work to be free or expensive. (At that time I was writing some health columns and articles for no fee at all and spending a big chunk of my income on sending out free books about animal experimentation to schools. I sent multiple copies of three books I'd written about animal experimentation to every school in Britain. And my newspaper fees meant that I could speak at worthwhile events without ever asking for expenses.)

The editor pushed back her chair. The deputy editor pushed back his chair. They got up, without a word, and walked away (though on their way out they did pay for lunch).

And that, of course, is the ultimate negotiating ploy. You walk away from the deal in order to bring down the price. You walk out of the car showroom. Or whatever.

I stayed in the restaurant for a while and ordered another coffee. My strength was that I was tired and didn't mind if I stopped writing the column.

A month later I agreed to sign a contract for £100,000 a year plus a 12% annual raise and a variety of remunerative extras. (It was, I was assured, the highest fee in Britain for a columnist).

But no contract appeared.

One Wednesday morning I had a phone call from the features editor. 'We don't have any copy for next Sunday,' she said.

'I don't have a contract,' I pointed out.

She rang again the following day.

And I pointed out that I still didn't have a contract.

On the Friday, the editor sent a contract down from London with a motorcycle messenger. I then faxed over a column for the following Sunday.

Editors all have one thing in common: like captains on a ship, they like to be in total control.

The added extra to this anecdote is that since exposing the covid fraud at the beginning of 2020, I have been totally blacked by the mainstream media for the modern crime of telling too much truth, and since then my total income from journalism has been approximately £0.

Crooks

'Crooks are honest men – they have to be, when you think of the deals they do with each other and that they daren't put anything in writing. You couldn't run an underworld for five minutes with the cheating that goes on in big business: breaking contracts, sub-standard goods, fighting law-suits.' – *Gavin Lyall*

J.M.W.Turner

Joseph Turner is arguably the greatest ever British painter (which means that I think he's the greatest but some argumentative souls prefer Stubbs, Constable or Gainsborough). He produced more than 20,000 paintings which he bequeathed to the English public. When not dossing down at Petworth House, he lived in a series of London pubs. He was once accused of charging too much for a painting and was taken before a local magistrate. The prosecutor asked Turner how long it had taken him to create the painting. Turner turned to the judge and replied: 'All my life, m'lord.' (The same response is attributed to Whistler, who came later, and one of the Bellini family, who came much earlier. But it sounds like Turner so Turner gets the credit.)

The First Garage Sale

Emperor Caligula, often hard up, organised a sale of unwanted bric a brac and to ensure a good price decided that he would be the auctioneer. All members of the imperial court had to attend and buy Caligula's junk at high prices. One poor fellow fell asleep, and Caligula decided that every time the man's head nodded he had bid. At the end of the auction, the fellow found that he had bought the equivalent of £2 million worth of Caligula's unwanted rubbish.

Car Travails

When I was a GP in the 1970s and 1980s, I regularly visited many patients at home (doctors did that in those days). The constant stopping and starting, and getting in and out of the car, resulted in my car door hinges failing regularly. And I needed to have the exhaust system replaced regularly too, because cars don't like lots of short journeys.

Jewels

After my mother died it was some months before I remembered that I hadn't seen her rings, locket and other jewellery. I went back to the nursing home where she died. A member of the staff opened a cupboard, took a brown envelope from a pile of similar envelops and handed it to me. 'We meant to let you know these were here,' she said, with a straight face.

Secrets of Surviving after Sixty

1. Always hold onto the bannisters when going up or down stairs.
2. Eat only when you are hungry and eat small, regular meals rather than huge meals which are difficult to digest.
3. Always assume that all health care professionals are planning to kill you.
4. Wear well-fitting, solid, supporting shoes with non-slip soles – both indoors and out of doors.
5. Never run anywhere – that's what children are for.
6. By all means change your career – but never retire. Statistics show that most people who die have retired.

Hippocratic Oath

The Hippocratic Oath is considered out of date. It may be. So here is my updated alternative: 'I promise to treat my patients with respect and to preserve their dignity at all times. I will treat all my patients as if they were my loved ones. I will treat my patients as I would like to be treated.'

Stays

In the 18th century, women were held together by 'stays' which consisted of metal or wooden rods between layers of stiffened linen, fastened with lacings. The stays were worn over a chemise to pull in the waist and give the wearer more shape. The wearer of a corset could hardly breathe or speak. The invention of the metal eyelet hole in 1828 made it possible to lace tighter and make waists smaller. Whalebone eventually took over from iron and wood and as a result the whaling industry boomed.

Brevity

'Brevity is the soul of lingerie' – *Dorothy Parker*

Guernica

The Basque town of Guernica was completely destroyed during the Spanish Civil War. But it wasn't destroyed by either Franco's forces or by the Republicans. The town was destroyed by an aerial bombardment carried out by Nazi Germany's Luftwaffe and an Italian force. The bombing was requested by General Franco, and it seems likely that Hitler agreed to the bombing because he wanted to test the Nazi plan to use carpet bombing techniques to terrorise civilian populations and to demoralise the enemy. The destruction of the town was immortalised by Pablo Picasso in a huge painting called Guernica which was commissioned by the Republican Government of Spain. Up until the bombing of Guernica, Picasso had taken very little interest in the Civil War. The painting was poorly received by critics and public at the time but is now considered to be one of Picasso's greatest achievements. It is also regarded as a plea for peace and a condemnation of genocide.

Always go for the royalty

Back in the early 1980s I was approached to make a series of telephone tapes for a new service called 'The Telephone Doctor'. People could telephone a number and listen to me giving advice on a variety of subjects. Advertisements for the service appeared regularly in all the national newspapers and magazines. When I first met the entrepreneur who set up the service, he offered me a choice: he would either pay me £2,000 to record the tapes or pay me a royalty on the Telephone Doctor's income. I chose the royalty. I always prefer a royalty to a flat fee. It took me a week or so to write the scripts and two weeks to record them. I talked for twelve hours a day, every day and had no voice at the end of the sessions. But over the next few years I earned rather more than the set fee in royalties. I mention this only as encouragement for anyone faced with the same choice. I have always found it much better to take a royalty rather than a fee. And I have always insisted on retaining copyright and selling rights though, sadly, copyright theft is now endemic. (For the record I have always refused to charge fees for access to my website and always refused to accept advertising or sponsorship. And none of the 300 plus videos I made after the start of the covid fraud was monetised, and all were available for people to copy and share. I suspect that some people made a good deal of money out of sharing my videos!)

Riots

It is agreed by governments, police and the media that groups on the Far Right are responsible for all riots and rowdy demonstrations. Governments, the police and the media seem to believe that far Left groups always demonstrate peacefully, quietly, politely and calmly.

Crafty crooks

A couple I once met bought a huge, beautiful country house which they couldn't afford. They took out a massive mortgage. They then gave themselves a tenancy on the property. When the bank tried to take back the house the couple could not be removed because they had a watertight contract allowing them to stay there indefinitely.

Marriage

'A young man in our village refused to marry a girl he had made pregnant because his family said, quite accurately, that she was not a virgin.' – *Daniel J.Beddowes*

Justice

A prisoner in France shouted 'Justice, I want justice!' And the judge said sternly 'I would remind the prisoner he is in a court of law'.

Preservation
In 1903, Joseph Karwowski invented a way of preserving dead humans for eternity. He was given US Patent 748,284. The deceased is covered in a thick layer of water glass and then molten glass is moulded around him or her. The body is preserved for eternity and can be viewed at all times. Relatives who cannot afford to have a whole body preserved can just have a head preserved by the same process.

Books
'One single book can significantly change the reader's attitude and action to an extent unmatched by the effect of any other medium.' – *Central Intelligence Agency*

Achievement
I am disappointed that when I was a GP I never managed to say (to a night time caller): 'Take two aspirin and ring me in the morning'. But I am cheered that I did once manage to say: 'Follow that car!' to a taxi driver. I was in London, staying at the Ritz for a Test Match at Lord's cricket ground. I came out of the hotel one morning to take a taxi to the cricket ground and saw that sitting in the taxi in front of me there was a man wearing a Panama hat decorated with a distinctive MCC coloured band. 'I'm going to say something I've always wanted to say – but with a twist,' I told the driver. He looked round at me, slightly puzzled. 'Follow that hat!' I said. The taxi driver laughed a good deal and, as I had hoped we would, we duly followed the man in the Panama hat to Lord's.

Denials
When official spokesmen speak, you should only ever believe their

denials. When official spokesmen deny something you can be confident that it is the truth.

Astor
'Unless we are very careful this welfare state will turn into a farewell state.' – *Lady Astor*

Average
We all spend an extraordinary amount of time dealing with dull, day to day activities. Anyone who lives to the age of 70 will have, on average, spent the following number of days on the following activities:
Cleaning their teeth – 75 days
Washing and bathing – 450 days
Going to the loo – 150 days
Sleeping – 8,516 days
Getting dressed and undressed – 300 days
Washing up (or loading and emptying dishwasher) – 450 days
Commuting – 1,500 days
Eating – 900 days
Cutting grass and weeding – 100 days
Washing clothes and ironing – 250 days

Kirkby, Liverpool
When I was 18-years-old, I spent a year in Kirkby, Liverpool as a Community Service Volunteer. No one knew what to do with me and I didn't quite know what to do with myself. At the time Kirkby was the toughest town in England. The local police station had locked gates and the walls were festooned with razor wire. Bus drivers wouldn't go into Kirkby after dark without a police escort. I did a survey of the town and found that huge numbers of old people were living there in tiny, nasty looking little flats. I went to the local

schools and recruited children to help decorate the flats. I warned the kids (who were aged about 11 to 16) that the local authority and the local trade unions didn't like what I was doing and that we could all get into serious trouble. They liked that. In fact I think that was what persuaded them to join me. (Even at 18 I knew that kids will do almost anything that is illegal, immoral, improper or disapproved of by people in suits. If you put an oil drum in a city centre, made a slit in the top and attached a notice saying: 'It is forbidden to put money in here', you'd have to empty the drum twice a day.) I then went to a local paint manufacturer and persuaded them to give me loads of paint. I used the local meals on wheels van (which I had been recruited to drive at lunchtimes, to deliver meals) to transport the paint and the kids to the flats. The main purpose of the exercise, of course, was to bring the young and the old together. Lots of them became friends. The kids helped the old people with chores, gardening and shopping. The old people told stories and became mentors. And then I left to go to medical school a million miles away. I never went back. I often wonder what happened to them all.

Pompous

Pompous people do have a long way to fall. When I was 12 we had one teacher, a bachelor, who was rude, aggressive and unbelievably pompous. I have never known anyone as full of his own sense of importance. One evening, while drunk, he drove his small motor car onto an even smaller, narrow bridge. The car was wider than the bridge. The car got stuck. The doors could not be opened. The fire brigade had to cut a hole in the car's roof in order to extricate our pompous teacher. And the bridge parapets had to be demolished in order to move the car. I'd like to report that the experience changed him and that he became patient, thoughtful and less self-important. But, perhaps wisely, he never returned to school. If he had been less pompous he would have had to put up with some jokes but the incident would have eventually been forgotten. But when a pompous individual is exposed to humiliation there can be no return.

Ages
Traditionally it was thought that a wife should be half husband – plus seven years. So if he is 100-years-old she should be 57. If he is 80, her ideal age is 47. If he is 50, she should be 32. If he is 40, she should be 27. If he is 30, she should be 22.

Decolletage
In 17th century France, ample ladies used the area below their decolletage as a storage area in which they would pack a handkerchief, a purse, and letters. The décolletage was used instead of a handbag. The amount of storage space depended on the size of the cleavage which depended on the size of the breasts.

Books
Readers used to buy books according to the cover and the title. A recent survey showed, however, that the average reader now gives a book one paragraph to catch their attention. If the first paragraph fails to excite them then the book will be returned or dumped.

Edward Dickens
Charles Dickens's youngest son was Christened Edward but he was known to the family as Plornishmaroontigoonter. A nice, catchy nickname that would doubtless save time in the mornings. 'Plornishmaroontigoonter, hurry up or you'll be late for school!'

Carrots
We throw carrots out onto the lawn every day. The wild rabbits come and eat them but they pay for their dinner by dancing and

ying a good deal. Unfortunately, our greenhouse is not far from the back door. When the glazier came to mend a broken window he wanted to know how the window had got broken. 'Oh, my wife threw a large carrot out for the rabbits,' I replied. To my surprise he said it was the first time he'd heard of anyone throwing a carrot through a window.

Dying
'Dying is a very dull, dreary affair. And my advice to you is to have nothing whatsoever to do with it.' – *Somerset Maugham, when he was dying.*

Additives
In both the US and the UK, foods which are heavily contaminated with additives (such as stabilisers, sweeteners and emulsifiers) make up more than half the daily calorific intake of the average citizen.

Difficult Doctors
Modern British GPs refuse to do many things that their predecessors used to do regularly. They refuse to syringe wax out of ears. They refuse to take blood samples or give injections. And they seem to delight in making life difficult for their patients. When Antoinette was prescribed tamoxifen for the treatment of her breast cancer, her GP refused to prescribe the stuff until the official letter from the hospital oncologist arrived – even though Antoinette had evidence that the drug had been prescribed. The letter from the hospital took weeks to arrive, of course. The GP could have telephoned the hospital but that would have been too much trouble. Modern GPs just do what they are required to do – and no more.

Licence

A widow in her mid-seventies, who lived in the country, went to see her doctor complaining of hearing loss. The doctor syringed her ears and removed a good deal of wax. Afterwards the woman complained that she felt dizzy. (This is quite normal after a syringing.) After ten minutes the dizziness disappeared and the woman drove home safely. But the GP wrote to the DVLA (the licensing authority for drivers) and reported that the woman had suffered from dizziness. The DVLA revoked the woman's licence and ignored requests to return it. The woman, not being able to drive, had to sell her lovely cottage and move into a flat in a nearby town. Her life was ruined.

Opticians

I am very wary of opticians. I have had three bad experiences. Ten years ago, one optician told me that I have cataracts. (I do not). Fifteen years ago an optician told me that I had macular degeneration but that she could sell me pills to cure me. I didn't have macular degeneration (and I didn't buy her very expensive pills). Twenty years ago a teenage boy in an optician's shop tested my visual fields as part of the examination of my eyes. He found massive gaps in my visual fields (a serious and scary health problem which can suggest a brain tumour). He was testing my visual fields with a white cursor on a blue screen. I cleaned the screen with my handkerchief and asked him to test my eyes again. This time there were no problems with my visual fields.

Claude Monet

Monet was painting his famous poplar trees in France when he discovered that the land was to be sold and the trees felled, and so he bought the land and saved the trees so that he could finish his paintings.

The Brain

Young people who are disdainful of the elderly should know that humans start to shrink in height at the age of 30, and by then their brains have been deteriorating for years. Indeed, by the time they reach 30 human beings are well into middle age.

Confidence tricksters

Confidence tricksters used to be imaginative and well thought of by other criminals.

One of the most successful confidence tricksters of the 20th century was a man called Joseph R.Weil (known, mysteriously, as the Yellow Kid) who flimflammed hundreds of victims or marks. He sold talking dogs (and then excused their silence with the excuse that they'd been stricken by laryngitis) and ran phony wiretap scams which he sold to gamblers as a way to beat the odds (as in the movie 'The Sting'). His most famous (or infamous) sting occurred when he was being taken to prison after he had been convicted. Weil managed to finesse $30,000 from the detective between the courthouse and the prison.

Weil once explained that the secret of his success was that all his victims had larceny in their hearts.

And then there was a Mr Howard Lee White, who was serving a sentence for forgery in the Fort Pillow State prison. He was released after the necessary papers had been delivered to the authorities. Sadly for the governor it transpired that Mr White had forged his own release papers. Subsequently, a man answering Mr White's description left a trail of cheques forged on the prison's account.

Then there are the confidence tricksters who offer to let us share their inheritance if we will send along our bank details, and the tricksters who want us to help them arrange a refund from the tax authorities (a refund which they will share with us).

Today, anyone with an email address will be bombarded with emails which purport to have been sent by a bank, by a delivery company or by the tax authorities. I don't do much online but I get several dozen of these every day. All offer to send me money if only I will send my bank details. These are often very cleverly done, with websites and emails which look extremely realistic (though there is often a clumsy spelling mistake somewhere in the email).

And these tricksters do not rely on the greed of their victims. They target the elderly and the vulnerable and they steal their savings. They aren't clever or entertaining. But they are annoying and unpleasant. And of course the people behind the scams all have one thing in common: they have larceny in their hearts. And they have no humanity.

Not all modern scams involve the internet, of course.

We live in a narrow, country lane which is closed to through traffic, and so we don't get many crooks and conmen knocking on our door and offering to trick us out of our chattels or our savings.

But now that I no longer look to be in the prime of life, we've had one or two strange experiences with people checking out to see if we are worth burgling. One young delivery driver stood looking up at our rather large house for quite a while before asking me if I owned the whole house, if I lived in it alone and if I had a dog. My answers to his questions clearly disappointed him. Another young driver who had to come into the house to help bring something heavy stopped and examined everything he passed. His questions were crass and rather obvious. 'Is this real silver?' 'Are those pictures valuable?' My replies ('No' and 'No') were obviously not what he was hoping to hear and he soon lost interest.

But these are small things.

The sadness is that the world is now, more than ever, controlled by a toxic melange of Zionist bankers, weapons makers, dishonest drug companies, greedy doctors, social media monstrosities, the BBC and an entirely out of control security industry.

Veronica Lake

When her career faltered, film star Veronica Lake (she of the peekaboo hairstyle) worked in a factory and as a cocktail waitress. After she died, her ashes remained with the undertaker for three years waiting for someone to pay the bill. Lake is probably best remembered for the wonderful 'Sullivan's Travels', which also starred Joel McCrea and was made by Preston Sturges (possibly the most underestimated auteur in American film history) and for three marvellous films she made with Alan Ladd – The Blue Dahlia, This Gun for Hire and The Glass Key. They are generally agreed to be the best of the film noir genre. (Well, I think they are and this is my book.) She did make another film (Saigon) with Ladd but it wasn't in the same genre or as successful. Ladd, of course, is best remembered for Shane – now generally recognised to be the greatest and most exquisitely romantic Western ever made and the prototype for scores of subsequent cowboy films.

Night Calls

When I pointed out to one young GP that their branch of the profession had lost the love of the public when they stopped doing night calls, she looked at me as if I were mad. 'Why should we get up and go out to work at night?' she asked, genuinely bewildered. 'You wouldn't expect an accountant to get up at 3 o'clock in the morning, would you?' She didn't understand the difference. I fear that most young doctors have little or no sense of vocation. Medicine is simply a good career.

Saving

Saving for the future is a very basic habit, popular among many animals. Just watch squirrels burying nuts in preparation for the winter.

Hedges

If there are ten species of tree in a hedge then the hedge is approximately 1,000 years old. The rule of thumb is that a hedge will contain one species of tree for every 100 years it has been in existence.

Clean Shoes

'As I polished my shoes last week, a young friend watched intently. He hadn't realised you could shine shoes yourself. 'Me and my friends,' he said, 'might buy one pair of shiny, black shoes for a wedding or funeral and keep them for rare occasions but then when they lose their shine we'd throw them away.' He looked at my Kiwi tin, brushes, cloth and vigorous polishing action with a kind of surprised interest, as one might observe a tribal rain dance.'
Matthew Parris

Ten Famous People Who Were Vehemently Opposed To Experiments on Animals

1. Henry David Thoreau
2. Abraham Lincoln
3. Albert Schweitzer
4. Albert Einstein
5. Charles Darwin
6. C.S.Lewis
7. Robert Browning
8. Mark Twain
9. George Bernard Shaw
10. Mahatma Gandhi

Prohibition

From January 1920, the sale of alcohol was banned in America. Before congress passed the Prohibition Act, many local laws had been enacted in various parts of America and some of these are doubtless still on the books. In St Louis it was made illegal to drink beer from a bucket while sitting on the pavement edge. In Ames, Iowa it was illegal for a man to drink more than three gulps of beer while in bed with a lover. In Lexington, Kentucky, legislators made it illegal to wear trousers which had a hip pocket big enough to hold a liquor flask. In Texas it is (or was) illegal to own the Encyclopaedia Britannica because it contained instructions on how to make booze. In Ojai, California it is illegal for a woman to stand within five feet of a bar counter while drinking. In Cushing, Oklahoma it was made illegal to drink beer while dressed only in underwear. In Nebraska, pub owners were only allowed to sell beer if they were also making and serving soup. Maine tried, and failed, to make it illegal to sell beer to anyone not standing up. Cold Springs in Pennsylvania passed a law which forced married men to have permission from their wives before they could buy alcohol. In Fairbanks, Alaska it was illegal to give any alcoholic beverage to a moose. And in Council Bluffs, Iowa it was illegal to climb a tree while intoxicated.

Fault
'If you limit your actions in life to the things that nobody can possibly find fault with, you will not do much.' – *Lewis Carroll*

The Orchard
'Before the Cherry Orchard was sold everybody was worried and upset, but as soon as it was all settled finally and once and for all, everybody calmed down, and felt quite cheerful.' – *Anton Chekhov*

Picking Your Disease
If you must get a disease, try to get a rare one and make sure you are admitted to a major teaching hospital. Doctors in teaching hospitals will happily let you die if you have something commonplace but they'll strive to keep you alive for as long as possible (if only as teaching material) if you have something unusual wrong with you.

Belief

'Most people will believe anything that tells against someone they dislike or flatters their self-esteem.' – *Hesketh Pearson*

Bravery

Bravery is a synonym for having absolutely no imagination.

Two Decades in Paris

Antoinette and I spent 20 years living part of the time in Paris (we used to travel backwards and forwards on Eurostar, and for several years were probably the company's best customers). To begin with the city was a delight and I enjoyed days masquerading as a flaneur (never kidding myself I could pass as a boulevardier). Sadly, over the years, everything deteriorated and life there became increasingly unpleasant and fractious. I would never live there again. Looking back, it is clear that the Parisians (or, rather, the people who work in Paris) are, almost without exception, crooked and greedy. When we bought our apartment, the seller and her notaire made a variety of promises (some of which were contractual) and then proceeded to break every single one of them without reason, explanation or apology. When we collected the keys, we found that even light fittings had been removed (with bare wires hanging from the ceiling) and that bathroom fittings had been taken out (we should be grateful, I suppose, that they left the taps). A sequence of workmen who were hired to do essential decorating, demanded money for materials and then disappeared, never to be seen again. We paid for 24 hour emergency cover for our heating and plumbing but found that we were lucky to get anyone to call at all. The company shut completely for the summer months. City inspectors of some kind on a routine check looking for termites, woodworm or democracy smashed down the wooden door to our cellar in the basement – and then just left it hanging off its hinges. They didn't even bother to apologise, let alone offer any compensation. (Inspectors regularly roam Paris looking for termites. We lived in the 7th arrondissement which is near the Eiffel Tower but the whole of Montmartre is said to be riddled with termites and it will only take an extra hungry couple of termites to bring Sacre Coeur crashing down.) Replacing the smashed cellar door cost us 1,500 euros – though we did replace it with a steel door which would have withstood a boot or even a sledgehammer. Towards the end of our 20 year stay there, the city of Paris demanded extra fees because we were not French. Our first bank allowed an internal crook to empty our bank account and only refunded the money when I threatened them with a lawyer and the media. The property agents, hired to look after the building, charged extortionate fees, were incredibly rude and completely ignored us whenever we tried to get in touch. The agents were responsible for hiring builders to look after the fabric of the building and to organise repairs. And they found cleaners for the public areas. They suddenly began to behave as though they owned the building. They made expensive decisions (and helped themselves to 20% of the contractor's fee) and organised alterations which we were ordered to pay for. The City itself had become overbearing and bureaucratic. For twenty years we tried everything we could think of to have the demand for the local taxes to be sent to an address in England. We spent hours in the local town hall filling in forms. And for twenty years we struggled to persuade the authorities to stop billing us for a television licence we didn't need because we didn't have a television. France used to be fairly free and easy but the country became insane and petty. For example, a pregnant woman was fined 60 euros for walking the wrong way at a metro station in Paris. And I wonder how many tourists know that it is now illegal to take photographs of the Eiffel Tower at night. The company which owns the Tower has the copyright on pictures of the Tower when it is lit. Utility companies dug underneath all the buildings in our arrondissement and removed vast quantities of rock. When they'd finished they replaced the rock with sand. It was, therefore, not surprising that when we sold the apartment the whole six storey building had developed huge cracks, not just in the plaster but in the once solid stone structure. At first we reassured ourselves that our building wouldn't fall down because it was one of a row of similarly sized buildings. And then we realised that all the other buildings had developed the same cracks in their stonework – ragged cracks so deep you could put your hand inside them. Just about every street in the arrondissement was much the same. In a year or two's time a whole arrondissement will crumble into the street. Was this done deliberately to expedite new planning rules? Or a simple act of stupidity? (To be fair, this sort of stupidity is not confined to France. In Devon, England the council sent huge machinery onto a cliff road to mend potholes. Two days later the road collapsed into the sea. No one accepted responsibility. The council probably blamed global warming and Brexit. In the same county, workmen from a utility company dug rock out of a road where they were hunting for utility cables and pipe. When they'd finished they took away the rock they'd removed and replaced it with sand. Within a month the road had developed a noticeable dip. Removing rock and replacing it with sand now appears to be standard practice.) When we came to sell our Parisian apartment, we were tricked and lied to more times than I can remember and afterwards, the notaire we were paying was officially reprimanded for his extraordinary behaviour. It took days to obtain the money we had been paid for the sale of the apartment.

Genius

'When a true genius appears in the world, you may know him by this sign; that the dunces are all in confederacy against him.' – *Jonathan Swift*

The Pirate

Pirate radio stations first appeared off the coast of England in the 1960s. Disc jockeys played round the clock pop music to the delight of millions of listeners who were fed up with the dull diet of old-fashioned band music being dished up by the BBC. Determined to close down the pirates, the Government introduced the Marine Offences Act on 14th August 1967. Just a handful of disc jockeys (including Johnnie Walker and Robbie Dale) remained on board. Then a new young presenter appeared. A television engineer called Chris Cary, who broadcast as Spangles Muldoon, arrived at the mv Mi Amigo, the ship from which Radio Caroline was broadcasting.

But he managed to arrive without a passport. He couldn't go back to England (because the ship was broadcasting illegally) and he couldn't go to Holland (where the tenders supplying the ship were based) so he was stuck on board. Needing a break he persuaded fans in a pleasure boat to smuggle him back to England where he obtained a passport. He then 'borrowed' a local council rowing boat and rowed the three and a half miles to the mv Mi Amigo. But Muldoon had left the ship without the captain's permission and had to stay bobbing up and down in his rowing boat, with a rope tied to the Mi Amigo's anchor chain, until Robbie Dale and Johnnie Walker managed to persuade the captain to allow him back onto the ship.

Smug
'Being smug is one of the compensations of getting old.' – *C.P.Snow*

Young
'When I was a young man I observed that nine out ten things I did were failures. I didn't want to be a failure so I did ten times more work.' – *George Bernard Shaw*

Medical students
Medical students used to be allowed to have fun. Filling the senior surgeon's rubber operating Wellington boots with cold water or ice cubes was a favourite pastime. Wheelchair races down hospital corridors were popular after midnight, when there were fewer innocents around to be injured. Filling filing cabinet drawers with fire extinguisher foam was considered as essential a part of the student's progress as being able to name the twelve cranial nerves (and their pathways) or being able to identify one of the eight bones of the wrist simply by feel. Taking doors off their hinges and switching them around so that keys did not fit was an excellent pastime for rare dull evenings and undoubtedly enlivened the lives of

administrators on dull Monday mornings. And lifting the surgical registrar's small motor car over a hedge and placing it on the lawn belonging to the matron wasn't just tolerated but expected. A colleague of mine (who later became an eminent psychiatrist) once helped himself to a bus when he wanted to get back to his flat and found that the official bus service had finished. (He left the bus outside his flat, making life simple for the police.) The medical school dean had a quiet word with the superintendent in charge of the local traffic police and no more was said. And when the traffic police needed road signs and cones they would call in at our flat and borrow what they required. They would, in due course, return what they had borrowed. When I ran a discotheque in the middle of Birmingham, I borrowed the medical school epidiascope and projector so that I could show medical slides and black and white Buster Keaton movies on the ceiling. (I always returned them the following morning.) Any of these activities would today result in disgrace, rustication and eternal banishment. Pranks and genial misbehaviour were regarded as essential stress relievers for students coming face to face, for the first time, with blood, illness and death. Sadly, today's administrators seem to have lost their sense of humour completely. The medical profession is poorer for it. It is no wonder that today's young doctors are a dull and timid lot.

Spending time

'This spending of the best part of one's life earning money in order to enjoy a questionable liberty during the least valuable part of it, reminds me of the Englishman who went to India to make a fortune first, in order that he might return to England and live the life of a poet.' – *Henry David Thoreau*

Clothes

Clothes carry the scent of sadness more than we realise. Some people give away or even burn the clothes they were wearing when they received bad news. This may help to cauterise the unhappy mood.

Strikers
Strikes were common surprisingly during the Great War. Enlisted soldiers, knowing that their chances of surviving another week were poor, read in their newspapers that workers in munitions factories were regularly going on strike (often for the most trivial of reasons). The result, of course, was that millions of hours of work were lost – and much ammunition that could have produced was not made. Soldiers facing death for a shilling a day had little sympathy with the strikers.

Loneliness
'Loneliness and the feeling of being unwanted is the most terrible poverty.' – *Mother Teresa*

Laughter
He who laughs last hasn't much of a sense of humour.

Hats
The civilised world came to an end when men and women stopped wearing hats on a regular basis.

No surprise
Live each day as if it were your last and one day you will be ready and not much surprised.

Pythagoras
'For as long as man continues to be the ruthless exploiter of other sentient beings, he will never know peace or joy, for as long as man massacres animals, men will kill each other, indeed, he who sows the seeds of torture and pain will never know real love, peace, health or happiness.' – *Pythagoras*

Home Buying
You should never buy a flat in the city on a wet, cold day. Anything which is warm and cosy will look wonderful. If you feel happy in a flat when it is a sunny day you will like it whatever the weather. The converse is true for the countryside. You should always buy on a cold, wet day. If you like a cottage in a howling gale, on a miserable day, with water dripping off the trees and mud everywhere then you will be far more likely to love it on a sunny day. And never buy a home that is so isolated that you cannot, in an emergency, walk, limp, hobble or cycle to a nearby shop. Do not rely on the future availability of public transport and do not rely on owning, and being able to drive, a vehicle of your own.

Best Film Noir Movies
Mask of Dimitrios
Glass Key
Blue Dahlia
Maltese Falcon

Under 30s
'Blind ambition, a burning sense of righteous entitlement, toxic self-satisfaction and misplaced trust are endemic among the under 30s

and likely to get worse rather than better. The mixture causes disappointment, disruption and will produce a collapse of everything previously regarded as essential for a functioning society.' – *Jack King*

Champagne

The French invariably claim to have invented champagne. Indeed, the European Union has given France the rights to the 'methode champenoise'. No wine maker living outside the limited Champagne region of France is allowed to use the name 'champagne' to describe their produce.

But the French didn't invent champagne.

Champagne was invented by a self-taught English scientist called Christopher Merrett who came from the cider producing West Country. Born in 1614, Merrett devised two techniques which were fundamental for manufacturing champagne; and he did it decades before the Benedictine monk Dom Perignon, who is usually given the credit for inventing the most luxurious of luxury wines.

Merrett used techniques from the cider industry to control the second fermentation process which makes wine fizzy.

It was in 1662 that Merrett gave a scientific paper to the Royal Society in London in which he described adding vast quantities of sugar and molasses to wine made it taste 'brisk and sparkling'.

It wasn't until 30 years later that Dom Perignon's work at the Abbey of Hautvillers at Epernay officially started the vast champagne industry.

It was also Merrett who invented the stronger glass which is needed to stop the bottle exploding when it contains champagne. In a publication entitled *The Art of Glass* he explained how bottles could be made stronger by adding iron, manganese or carbon to the molten mixture. Early French champagne makers recognised Merrett's contribution and described the bottles they used as being made of verre Anglais (English glass).

So, champagne is English, not French.

And, once again, the European Union is wrong.

Criticism
The best way to avoid criticism is to keep quiet and do nothing. But what sort of life is that?

Writing
'Writing is an act of love. If not, it is merely paperwork.' – *Jean Cocteau*

Bottom line
With the exception of death, the bottom line is hardly ever as bad as you think it's going to be.

Truth
'During times of universal deceit, telling the truth becomes a revolutionary act.' – *George Orwell*

Rules
People in authority are unable to think for themselves. At one point in our lives we had three homes and so I tried to register a car with a correspondence address which we use. My thought was that if I received a summons for speeding or parking or some other offence which I didn't know I'd committed, the paperwork would be sent on to me wherever we were at the time. However, the DVLA refused to accept the correspondence address and insisted that the car could only be registered at our permanent address. This meant that we had to pick one address as being 'permanent', knowing that if we were at another address for, say, a month, then the police summons would sit on our hall carpet for a month and I would get into trouble. The

ot be moved from their irrational, bureaucratic

John Ruskin
'There is hardly anything in the world that can be made a little worse and sold a little cheaper and the people who consider price alone are that man's lawful prey.' – *John Ruskin*

The Rich
'The rich are always afraid.' – *Pearl S. Buck*

Inventions
Most people overlook, or take for granted, the everyday things in life. We give much praise to the inventors who gave us computers, telephones and the internet but our lives have been far more dramatically improved by the inventions of the washing machine, the refrigerator and the vacuum cleaner (without which the emancipation of women would have been a much harder and longer struggle). And why does no one ever celebrate the forgotten inventors who gave us hats, gloves, bags and, simplest but most useful of all, the humble pocket? All of these things we take for granted. The most important inventions were the wheel, writing paper, pencils, the bicycle and the internal combustion engine.

The Funniest Book Ever Written
Three Men in a Boat by Jerome K. Jerome

C.S.Lewis
You wouldn't condemn a dog on a newspaper report.

Artificial Intelligence
'Using the over promoted AI is like having a teenager helping you. You have to check everything it does and then do it yourself anyway.' – *Jack King*

Luck
'We must believe in luck for how else can we explain the success of those we don't like?' – *Jean Cocteau*

Youth
'To get back my youth I would do anything in the world except take exercise, get up early or be respectable.' – *Oscar Wilde*

Minutes
Look after the minutes as carefully as you look after the pennies and the hours, like the pounds, will look after themselves.

Yes Men
'I don't want any yes-men around me. I want everybody to tell me the truth, even if it costs them their jobs.' – *Samuel Goldwyn*

The Shopping Race
In Amsterdam, Holland a running race for women was devised with the motto 'Shopping is a Sport.' Contestants had to wear stiletto heeled shoes with heels a minimum of three and a half inches high. The course was 380 yards long.

Battle of Britain
The most extraordinary board game ever devised is called 'Battle of Britain'. The game recreates the epic air battle of early WWII. Here are the instructions: 'The planes of Hitler's Third Reich hurled themselves at the embattled Great Britain. Two players command either the German Luftwaffe or the British royal Air Force. The German commander chooses missions, moves his air groups over Britain and makes bombing runs against vital targets. The British commander decides where and when to hazard his meagre fighter forces and, in the Advanced Game, picks how best to use his factories to rebuild his defences and fighter squadrons.' The aim for the 'German' player is to win the game and the war. If the 'British' player can destroy the Luftwaffe and outlast the German attacks then Britain wins. The game consists of 21 plastic planes and bases, 1 sheet of flight labels, 1 map board, 4 RAF Group Displays, 48 RAF Squadron cards, 112 Luftwaffe Squadron Cards, 35 mission cards, one sheet of counters, 1 rulebook, 6 white RAF dice, 6 black Luftwaffe dice.'

I believe that the game is the most complicated ever compiled. The A4 size rule book consists of 16 pages and I found it close to incomprehensible.

Fay Taylour
Fay Taylour was one of the earliest female racing drivers. In 1934, she came second in the Autumn Ladies Mountain Handicap race but at the end of the race was enjoying herself so much that she decided not to stop. Officials watched in astonishment as Ms Taylour, driving a Penn-Hughes 2.6 Alfa Romeo drove on and on. Flags were

waved and officials became increasingly distressed. Eventually, a race marshall stood in her path and Ms Taylour put on the brakes and stopped. Sadly, she was fined and excluded.

Fear
'Nothing is terrible except fear itself.' – *Francis Bacon*

Too Many Shoes
After a couple moved into a farmhouse in Lincolnshire they started to find shoes dumped at the end of their driveway. Over the next few months, around 30 pairs of footwear appeared out of nowhere. Some were designer brands, others were worn. There were toddler's shoes and roller blades. Some of the shoes still had price tags attached. Video surveillance showed an elderly couple were tossing the shoes into the driveway. After publicity the shoes stopped appearing.

Ideas
'No grand idea was ever born in a conference.' – *F Scott Fitzgerald*

The Ultimate Boys' Toy
In the early 20th century Armstrong, Whitworth & Co, one of Britain's leading producers of locomotives, automobiles and armaments, made a miniature silver railway, complete with rails, engine, tender and carriages, which was designed to run around a long banqueting table. The train carried port and cigars and was designed to stop automatically when a guest reached out for any of the contents carried on the train.

Most Inspirational Movie
Stand Up Guys

Trivia
It is because millions only ever concern themselves with the trivia – the best way to make a padded pelmet and three ways to eradicate moss from your lawn – that our world has become the obscenely barbaric place it is.

Big Appetites
According to a 19th century publication called *The Modern Housewife*, a 19th century gentleman would, in his lifetime consume just over 33 tons of food, including:
30 oxen
200 sheep
200 lambs
50 pigs
40 deer
500 hares and rabbits
1,200 chickens
300 turkeys
150 geese
400 ducklings
263 pigeons
1,400 partridges, pheasant and grouse
600 woodcock and snipe
600 wild duck, widgeon and teal
450 plovers, ruffes and reeves
800 quails, ortolans, dotterols, guillemots and other foreign birds
120 guinea fowl
10 peacocks
360 wild fowl
120 turbot

140 salmon
120 cod
260 trout
400 mackerel
300 whiting
800 soles and slips
400 flounders
400 red mullet
200 eels
150 haddock
400 herrings
5,000 smelt
100,000 whitebait
20 turtles
30,000 oysters
1,500 lobsters or crabs
300,000, prawns, shrimps, sardines and anchovies
500 lb of grapes
360 lb of pineapple
600 peaches
1,400 apricots
240 melons
100,000 plums, greengages, apples, pears
Several million cherries, strawberries, raspberries, currants, mulberries, walnuts, chestnuts, figs, plums
5,475 lb of vegetables
2,434 lb of butter
684 lb of cheese
21,000 eggs
4.5 tons of bread
Half a ton of salt and pepper
Two tons of sugar
49 hogsheads of wine
1,368 gallons of beer
584 gallons of spirits
342 gallons of liqueur
2,394 gallons of coffee, cocoa, tea, etc.
304 gallons of milk
2,736 gallons of water

Oil
Oil was created by God with the help of a process called photosynthesis – which requires sunshine. And so it is no exaggeration to say that petrol and diesel driven vehicles are the only truly solar powered forms of transport available to us.

Best Film about Money
The Big Short

Dog bites
'If a dog bites someone surely the owner, not the dog, should be destroyed.' – *Noral Johnson*

Funniest Book Series
The Jeeves and Wooster books by P.G.Wodehouse

Perspective
It is important (but sometimes difficult) to see things in perspective. It may help to know that nearly half the people in the world do not have the kind of clean water and sanitation services that were available two thousand years ago to the citizens of ancient Rome. And many people want to keep things that way.

In Your Head

'It doesn't matter where you live – where you live is really in your head.' – *Henry David Thoreau*

Christmas Trees

In 1999, Antoinette and I bought an artificial Christmas tree. We purchased it at a branch of Woolworth and it cost £9.99. It is a very good tree and we have no plans to replace it, but in 2020 we decided that we had so many ornaments that we needed a second tree. The second tree cost £49.99, is smaller and is nowhere near as well made. Life in a nutshell.

School Daze

When I was a teenager, fountain pens were considered unacceptably high tech, guaranteed to destroy handwriting and to turn the users into namby pamby softies. Everyone I knew used a wooden pen with a replaceable nib. The wooden handles were distributed at the start of the school year, together with a nib, a pencil and an eraser. When the metal nib became crossed and started writing double, the teacher would replace it from a box in the drawer of his desk. The replacement would usually already have a crossed nib. Almost everything I wrote from the age of 11 to 18 was written in double joined up writing. Pens were dipped into an inkwell, built into the top right hand corner of each desk, and the inkwells were refilled at the end of each day by the ink monitor. The pens, adapted with a little chewing gum, were used as darts and paper pellets soaked in the ink made wonderful ammunition for rubber band wars.

 Milk monitors, selected by form masters, were responsible for bringing in and supervising the distribution of the day's supply of third of a pint of milk per pupil. On cold days the milk would freeze and bottles would be handed out with three inches of solid milk, capped with a silver foil top, protruding from the top of the bottle. For warmer days we were given little plastic devices which enabled us to press in the silver foil and therefore remove it from the bottle. Someone is doubtless selling these on eBay for large sums of money.

Complicated mathematical sums were worked out with the aid of log books and slide rules which no one understood but which everyone accepted as being essential. Calculators were the size of typewriters and were found only in the posher retail establishments.

Bicycles, not motor cars, were the preferred mode of transport. I used to leave mine for hours without ever locking it. I don't think I knew anyone who had a lock for a bicycle.

What am I worth?

While looking for something else on the internet I found a site claiming that my net worth is $28 million. This came as a surprise to me. It turned out that the site's management had based their evaluation on my social media presence. Since I have never had a presence on any social media site I can only assume that other people's comments have been used to produce this number. I found a second site which estimated my net worth at $60 million. But, lo, I did a little searching and found another site which stated, quite firmly, that my net worth is $600,000. Once again it seems that the number is based on my non-existent social media presence. How curious life has become.

Marco Polo

In the story of his adventures, Marco Polo describes his time at the court of the Great Khan. Marco was 17 when he left home in Venice. It had taken him four years to reach the home of the Great Khan. Here Marco Polo describes how the Great Khan moved between his palaces.

'In the very midst of his subjects, went, in magnificent state, Kublai Khan himself. He was perched on the back of an enormous white elephant, down whose huge leathery sides hung draperies of cloth of gold and silver, worked with the symbols of the Buddhist faith in many dazzling colours. Above these draperies appeared a splendid pavilion, supported by slender and beautifully carved pillars of sandal-wood and other aromatic woods. It was curtained in the richest silk; above it rose a little dome, plated with silver, and surmounted by many brilliant plumes, that waved and nodded high in the air.

'Within the pavilion was a throne which was one blaze of burnished gold and which was supplied with a large, soft cushion, as large and soft as a feather bed. Its arms were carved tiger's heads, the eyes of the tigers being immense emeralds; and upon this throne sat, or rather reclined, the mighty monarch of Cathay.

'On a cushion on one side of the Khan, reposed a beautiful, young girl, one of the most recent and well beloved of his many wives; while on the other side of the throne, and chained to its leg, sat a small but handsomely spotted leopard, the Khan's favourite pet.

'All around the elephant that bore the Khan were other elephants, which carried his wives and principal courtiers, who were being constantly fanned by their dusky slaves with fans made of peacock's feathers.

'The journey from the imperial hunting grounds to Kambalu, the capital of Cathay, occupied several weeks; for the two places were some hundreds of miles apart.'

'The Khan had a large number of wives. Of these four were held in higher honour than the rest, and were called Empresses. Each of these Empresses was entitled to take the Khan's name and each had a separate court of her own, with a palace all to herself. Each Empress was attended by no less than ten thousand persons, among whom were three hundred of the loveliest maidens of Cathay. It was a great honour to belong to an Empress's court, and all the young girls of the country were anxious to be chosen. By his four Empresses, the Khan had twenty two sons and by his other wives, no less than twenty five more.

Later in his account, Marco Polo describes his travels on a ship travelling along the western coast of the Indian continent. The coast of Malabar swarmed with pirates who were in the habit of signalling to one another when a merchant vessel appeared. Lights on the corsair ships telegraphed the news of a coming prize so that the poor merchantmen had little chance of escape. The merchant ships were, therefore, strongly armed and manned. Marco Polo was told that the pirates, on seizing a ship, would take all the goods but did not harm the crew. Instead they said: 'Go and get another cargo, so that we may catch you again and rid you of it.'

Old Age
Age brings wrinkles, deafness and wobbles but it also brings perspective and perspicacity. I know what it's like to be young but I don't have the foggiest idea how it feels to be as old as I'll be tomorrow.

Don't Listen
'When I started writing seriously, I made the major discovery of my life – that I am right and everybody else is wrong if they disagree with me. What a great thing to learn. Don't listen to anyone else, and always go your own way.' – *Ray Bradbury*

Life isn't Fair
The phrase 'Life isn't fair' is too often used as an excuse. It should be regarded as an impetus; a signal for action.

Entitled
The young and entitled collect grievances, resentments and disappointments in the same way that their parents and grandparents collected stamps or cooking recipes.

Art
Any work of art (whether it be a painting, a book, a play, a sculpture or a piece of music) will never be finished and must always be a work in progress.

Rationing
During the Great War, food was rationed and became so scarce that it was made illegal to throw rice at a wedding and unlawful to feed pigeons or stray dogs. After the Second World War, rationing continued in England for years after the end of the fighting and for years after rationing in Germany had been stopped.

Too much thinking
People who claim to be thinking things over before making a decision are invariably merely looking for a solid sounding excuse to justify a decision they have already made.

Adoption
'Polls show that most people don't approve of homosexuals being allowed to adopt children. But most people were never asked for their views. A goodly percentage would doubtless disapprove of homosexuals marrying in the church, if they were allowed a voice. But no one is allowed to ask the questions and so there is never any discussion. The result is simmering resentment and permanently established prejudice.' – *Will Cotter*

Dachau
The character played by George C. Scott in Paddy Chayefsky's film The Hospital is disgusted by the behaviour of the nurses and demands of a senior hospital employee: 'Where do you train your nurses, Dachau?'

    The trouble with health care today is that doctors and nurses are taught to regard patients as clients and, as with banks, brokers, car salesmen, insurance companies and utilities, the clients are merely fodder.

The Big Sleep

When the movie 'The Big Sleep' was being made, Bogart asked director Howard Hawks who had killed the chauffeur. Hawks realised he had no idea so he asked William Faulkner, who was one of the script writers. Faulkner confessed that he didn't know and suggested that they ring Raymond Chandler who had written the book on which the film was based. Chandler admitted that he didn't know either. In the end no one cared because it really didn't matter who had killed the chauffeur. The film's plot leaves viewers confused and bewildered. But it's a great movie and that's really all that matters.

Waste

We all waste too much of our lives and the way society is organised these days means that we are forced to keep wasting time. So far this month I've wasted many hours trying to persuade my pension company to continue paying my pension (out of the money they are supposed to look after for me) and our absurdly incompetent energy supplier to allow me to pay them via the direct debit I set up three years ago, but which they still seem to find too complicated to understand. The most valuable commodity any of us has is time and every minute that is stolen from us is valuable.

Fun

There is a line in the BBC film series of 'Smiley's People' in which a German cathouse proprietor called Claus Kretzschmar, talking to George Smiley, tells the straight-laced spy: 'Maybe you should have had more fun in your life.'

Ruefully, Smiley agrees with this. 'Maybe I should,' he admits.

I can't help thinking we should have had more fun. We have both worked hard; organising and running numerous campa

The saying 'Living well is the best revenge,' is usu
F. Scott Fitzgerald but he stole it from a 17th century
George Herbert.

And it is, perhaps, our right and our duty to take pleasure gratefully and without guilt.

My Father's Luncheon

My 87-year-old father parked his car (quite legally) and went into a hotel to have lunch. While he was enjoying his meal, the manager tottered over and told him that the police wanted to speak to him. My father abandoned his meal and struggled down the steps to the roadside. Another motorist had nudged my father's car while he was parking. There was no damage to either car. My father's car was parked perfectly legally. The police were in the vicinity only because they had been called to another minor traffic accident. My father confirmed that there was no damage and was eventually allowed to go back into the hotel to finish his (by now cold and ruined) luncheon. A couple of weeks later he received a letter from someone in the local 'collisions department' of the constabulary informing him that the police had given themselves six months to decide whether or not to take legal action as a result of his collision. At the time of the offence, remember, he was sitting in a hotel eating his lunch while his car was parked outside. And, remember, there was no damage done to either vehicle and neither he nor anyone else had complained. He received further warnings about this non-existent incident and was, as a conscientious, law-abiding citizen unnerved by them. He knew he had done absolutely nothing wrong. But the police were, nevertheless, warning him about some unspecified legal action. And so he was desperately worried. Madness, utter madness.

Cholesterol

The whole of that part of the health care industry which is devoted to reducing cholesterol levels (with the aid of statins) is little more than confidence trick. There is no convincing evidence to show that reducing cholesterol levels is a good thing. Indeed, there is a good deal of evidence to show that reducing cholesterol levels is a bad thing and that the drugs used to lower cholesterol levels are a very bad thing. Those are not ideas which the medical profession and the pharmaceutical industry want to see widely disseminated. It is far more convenient and profitable to continue with the current extremely profitable myth.

Bureaucracy

'Bureaucracy is a great machine operated by pigmies.' – *Honore de Balzac*

Trial by Ordeal

The Saxons were very superstitious people and when a member of a community had committed an offence they had to be exposed to an ordeal, rather than a trial. The accused would have to expose himself to danger. If he survived then he was considered innocent. (Women were also exposed to these ordeals.)

There were four ordeals, two by fire and two by water

1. The accused was forced to walk blindfolded and in bare feet over nine red hot iron ploughshares placed at unequal distances. In the unlikely event that he missed all the ploughshares, he was considered innocent.

2. The accused was forced to pick up a red hot iron in his hand. If he could hold it without being burned he was innocent.

3. The accused had to thrust a naked arm into a vessel full of boiling water. If it wasn't scalded then he was innocent.

4. The accused was thrown into deep water. If he stayed motionless but floated then he was innocent. If he thrashed about or struggled he was considered guilty. There was a variation on this theme for women accused of witchcraft. The accused would be thrown into deep water, with a rope round their waist and their right thumb tied to their left toe. If they sank they were innocent. If they

swam and survived they were guilty and burnt alive. An(
method of 'trying' witches was to weigh the accused aga
church Bible. If the woman on trial weighed more than t
was innocent. If the Bible was the heavier then the woman was guilty.

Trial by ordeal lasted until the reign of King John but for witches it extended until the reign of King James 1.

Patron Saint of the Innocent

St Dominic is the patron saint of innocents who are falsely accused of crime. He is often depicted in icons holding a book, though the title of the book is not usually made clear.

Free Money is Popular

Scientists conducted an experiment to find out what happened when people were given free money. The study involved 3,000 low income Americans aged 21-40 who were randomly assigned to receive either $1,000 a month for three years or just $50 for taking part in the experiment. The experiment was conducted to test the popular proposal that everyone should be given a 'universal basic income'. To widespread astonishment, the results showed that when people are given free money they work less and play more.

If

In 2018, students at Manchester University scrubbed Kipling's poem 'If' from a wall. I am not sure whether they were offended by Kipling, the poem or the wall. But they were clearly offended by something. Maybe they would have been happier if they'd actually read the poem.

cared

'Health service staff in the UK are regularly threatened with reprisals if they speak out about injustices and bad practices. That's bad enough. But what's even worse is that the vast majority keep quiet when they are threatened.' – *Daphne Baker*

Paul Klee

During World War I, the Swiss-German artist Paul Klee was assigned to a military airfield near Munich. Klee's job was to paint lozenge patterns on German biplanes so they would blend in with the sky. (If anyone can find one of the aeroplanes he painted, it is now probably worth more than the entire German air-force.)

William Tell

William Tell, who lived in the later years of the 13th century and the early years of the 14th century, is remembered around the world for shooting an apple off his son's head with a crossbow. The story suggests that having cut the grass and played a little one-a-side football, Tell decided to liven up the afternoon by picking up a bruised windfall and using his son for target practice ('Stand still, son, or your mother will kill me.'). But this is grossly unfair. Tell was ordered to shoot the apple off his son's head by Albrecht Gessler, an Austrian. When Tell took two bolts from his quiver, Gessler asked him what the second bolt was for. Tell replied that if he killed his son he would use the second bolt to kill him, Gessler. Not surprisingly, this rather annoyed the Austrian who locked him up. However, William Tell later succeeding in killing Gessler – with a crossbow, of course. Killing Gessler encouraged the Swiss to rise up and as a result, Switzerland became independent. Tell is, of course, the Swiss equivalent of the English folk hero, Robin Hood.

Def Leppard

Rick Allen is the drummer with the rock band Def Leppard. In 1985 his left arm was amputated. Encouraged by support from friends, family, fans and the rest of the band, Allen carried on playing the drums – with just his right arm.

Pleasure

Antoinette was waiting for an operation. We had a letter from the hospital. It began, 'I have pleasure in offering you a telephone pre-operative assessment'.

'Pleasure!'

It's the sort of greeting you expect when you've won £25 on the Premium Bonds or been awarded a chance to have a free assessment for double glazing.

The strange thing is that no one at the hospital seems to think that it is odd to offer pre-operative assessments by telephone – even though they are utterly useless and, therefore, extremely dangerous. In the bad old days no patient went into an operating theatre without a full medical examination. Hearts and lungs were auscultated, abdomen was palpated, blood pressure was taken and so on.

These days they do a superficial and entirely useless examination by telephone.

Progress.

Hiding

I can understand why people reject treatment they have been advised to accept.

When I was a GP I had a young patient who had a positive cervical smear. I saw her and told her that she had to go to the hospital. She refused. I wrote to her. She refused. I went to her home. She saw me and listened to me but still refused to go to the hospital. I sent the district nurse round. I telephoned. She refused. I wrote again. She never went. She died two years later.

She could have probably been saved. But what can you do? I

could hardly drag her out of her home, put her into the car and take her screaming to the hospital. Or should I have done that? I didn't know then and I still don't know.

But now, at last, I think I do understand why she didn't want to be treated.

Rules
'Any fool can make a rule – and every fool will mind it.' – *Henry David Thoreau*

My Favourite Thriller and Espionage Writers (in order)
1. Adam Hall
2. Eric Ambler
3. Gavin Lyall
4. Philip Kerr
5. Brian Freemantle
6. John Buchan
7. Dornford Yates
8. Charles McCarry
9. Derek Haas
10. Laurence Block
11. Donald E. Westlake aka Richard Stark
12. Robert Campbell
13. Graham Greene
14. Colin Egleton
15. Sapper
16. Robert B Parker
17. Andrew Vachss
18. Len Deighton
19. Robert Littell
20. Micky Spillane
21. Rex Stout

(I've read everything by John Le Carre and Ian Fleming but neither appears on this list I'm afraid, though films of their books have been hugely successful and enjoyable. And I've read everything by Dick Francis and Colin Dexter – but I don't re-read their books. The authors on this list I do re-read.)

Modern culture

'In his influential 1895 book *Degeneration*, the Hungarian doctor and intellectual Max Nordau had argued that modernist culture – from the ideas of Nietzsche, Ibsen and Zola to the work of the French Impressionists – was an outgrowth of the social and racial decline of the late 19th century. In his strained interpretation, the rapidity of modern urban life – 'the shocks of railway travelling…the perpetual noises and the various sights in the streets of a large town…the constant expectation of the newspapers' – had led to the physical degradation of human populations over time, a process that in turn was producing rampant crime, addiction and deviant behaviour, including subversive new forms of cultural expression.' – *Hugh Eakin* (Roughly a century later I devised the term 'toxic stress' to describe the way that background stresses were responsible for much mental and physical ill health.)

Public opinion

'One should as a rule respect public opinion in so far as it is necessary to avoid starvation and to keep out of prison, but anything that goes beyond this is voluntary submission to an unnecessary tyranny, and is likely to interfere with happiness in all kinds of ways.' – *Bertrand Russell*

The Funniest Movies
Let it Ride
Red
The Producers (Gene Wilder version)

The sound of sheep

Driving through Devon I stopped for petrol. I was alone. I was alert, awake and not at all tired.

The only other vehicle at the petrol station was one of those huge lorries used to transport sheep from farms to abattoirs. The lorry was parked to one side – about twenty or thirty yards away from the petrol pumps.

As soon as I got out of my car I heard the sheep bleating in the lorry. The sound was clear and distinctive. As I filled my car with petrol the sound made by the sheep continued.

When I had finished filling my car I went into the kiosk and paid for the petrol. On my way back to my car I suddenly stopped, drawn towards the lorry. The baaing had become louder and more insistent. It suddenly occurred to me that one of the sheep might be in special distress. Animals in these lorries are crammed together so tightly that one sometimes gets a leg caught in between the slats of the lorry wall. Maybe I could help.

I walked over to the lorry and looked inside. As soon as I looked inside the baaing stopped. And I could see that the lorry was completely, utterly empty.

There was not one sheep inside it.

Nor were there any sheep anywhere else nearby. There were no other lorries and no sheep in nearby fields.

The explanation?

Could the lorry have still been carrying the pain of all those sheep who had been transported, in pain and anguish, to their death?

Whatever the explanation may be, this story is absolutely true.

Undeserved Compliments

People who don't know anything about medicine are invariably complimentary about the National Health Service – the UK's socialised health care system. Patients and relatives are usually quick to rebut criticisms by drawing attention to their own often contented

experiences. Sadly, the praise is rarely merited and is b
on faulty foundations – a mixture of misunderstandings
was done and what should have been done. It is worth
that most NHS staff admit that they would not want to be treated ...
the hospital where they work. It is a sad but undeniable fact that
those NHS staff members who can afford to do so choose to be
treated privately – outside the NHS. The General Medical Council,
and many unions for health service employees, provide private
health care insurance for their employees so that they do not have to
be exposed to the horrors of the NHS.

A Strange Conversation

I was coming out of our drive when a man approached me.

'You're not Hawkwind are you?' he said.

'No, I don't think so.' I replied.

'I didn't think so,' he said. 'I never liked Hawkwind.' And then he walked away.

It was a pretty curious conversation even for someone who has had a lifetime of rummy conversations.

Pensions

'Older pensioners in the UK receive much smaller pensions than younger pensioners. This, of course, is counter-intuitive and cruel because the older people get the more they are likely to need a little extra money for heating and so on. In 2024, men who were born before 6th April 1951 and women who were born before 6th April 1953 received £2,688.40 a year less than pensioners who were born after those dates. It's difficult to avoid the suspicion that giving the elderly less money is deliberately designed to kill them off and save the State the money spent on looking after them. The difference in the two types of pension has been growing for years and is constantly getting more and more significant. It is probably the biggest unreported scandal in modern Britain.' – *Jack King*

Cut Tyres

We had a 'visual health check' on our Maserati from the garage. The report contained these chilling words: 'Both Front Tyres Cut to Cord'. Both front tyres had to be replaced (though they had only done about 1,500 miles) because someone had deliberately cut deeply into them. Both cuts were on the inner part of the tyre and therefore pretty well invisible. The Maserati had a top speed of 180 mph. I shudder to think what would have happened if one of the tyres had burst as planned. The only modest consolation is that if they are trying to kill you then you must be doing something right.

Purbeck

In November 1943, villagers living in Tyneham on the Isle of Purbeck were told that they had 28 days to leave their homes because the area was needed for army training. All 102 homes in the village were evacuated. The departing villagers left a note on the church door which read: 'We have given up our homes where many of us have lived for generations to help win the war to keep men free. We will return one day and thank you for treating the village kindly.'

But the village wasn't treated kindly. The army shelled the village and left it in ruins. After the war, the Ministry of Defence compulsorily purchased the whole valley. Villagers spent decades trying to reclaim their land and what remained of their houses and cottages but successive governments stood firm – though no reason was given for their intransigence. Volunteers have done what they can to restore the village but it remains empty of human life.

Essential being

'However men may choose to regard me, they cannot change my essential being, and for all their power and all their secret plots I shall continue, whatever they do, to be what I am in spite of them.' –

Jean-Jacques Rousseau

Caine meets Wayne
In 1966, when he was a rising star, Michael Caine met John Wayne. 'Never wear suede shoes,' Wayne told Caine. 'Why?' asked Caine, puzzled. 'One day,' replied Wayne, 'you will be taking a pee and the guy next to you will see you, recognise you and say 'Michael Caine!' and he'll turn and piss all over your shoes.'

Looking Back
I was, so I'm told, the first 'agony uncle' on national television (on the BBC). And several centuries ago I wrote an agony column for a now defunct magazine for teenage girls. I then wrote an advice column for a Sunday newspaper. My columns were syndicated in magazines and newspapers around the world. My mail came in sacks and in languages I don't even recognise let alone understand. I received between 5,000 and 10,000 letters and phone calls every week. Strange days.

Thoughts
'I hate bureaucrats and administrators. I loathe grey men in suits. I despise politicians, lawyers and people who tell me what I can or cannot do. I am probably the only person in the world who has managed to annoy (and unite) the pin stripes of the orthodox medical establishment and the corduroy jackets of the alternative medicine establishment. Injustice and cruelty make me incandescent. I have never had a proper job of any kind. I am constantly in trouble, constantly being threatened and for ever being warned that unless I learn to compromise I will never have a successful career. I cannot cook, iron shirts, put up shelves or maintain motor cars. I am always losing things. I hate travelling and although I have for much of my life earned my living as a writer, I hardly ever visited the offices of

either the publishers or newspapers I worked for. I cannot understand or operate properly any of the sophisticated electronic equipment upon which I am dependent. I am soft hearted to a fault, sentimental and incurably romantic. I am, I know, extremely prickly. It is good to know one's faults. I am naive enough and innocent enough to have retained all my teenage dreams. I am sceptical about the promises made by the men (and women) in suits and white coats and cynical about the influence of big business on all our lives. I hate compromise and am ruthlessly unforgiving. I worry too much. But, on the other hand, there are some things that I can do. I can ride a bicycle and I can swim (though not at the same time). I can lay a hedge and I can remove an inflamed appendix. I can sew up a wound and remove the stitches when the wound has healed. It's not a lot. But it's a beginning, perhaps.' – *From Vernon Coleman's website, Devon 1994*

Appendix 1

The following essay appeared one Christmas in my column in *The People* newspaper:

Don't slump down in front of the television set just yet because I have a present for you. It's a present that will not wear out or go out of fashion. It doesn't need batteries and you don't have to queue up to exchange it. It is a present that may make you feel uncomfortable for a few minutes but will, if you accept it, last for ever and change your life.

All I ask from you, in return for the gift I want to give you, is a little indulgence and a few moments of your time.

Of course, there is a chance you may not need my present. So, before we go any further let me ask you whether you think you have done as much as you can with your life. If you knew that you had just five minutes to live would you be satisfied that you had done as much as you could with your allotted lifespan?

If you aren't quite sure then read on.

Because I'm going to give you a philosophy for life.

Most people are dead at twenty five: their ambitions, hopes and aspirations confined to acquiring a car with 'genuine' vinyl seats and a fully paid up pension plan. They won't be buried for another half a century but they are doing little more than killing time until life runs out. They watch life drift by; never grasping their destiny or taking control. Thoreau was right when he wrote that 'the mass of men lead lives of quiet desperation'.

How many of your friends do jobs that they hate – and then excuse themselves by arguing that they need the money to pay for the stuff with which they have littered their lives. (And how much of that stuff – paid for with blood, sweat and tears – is worth the price that has been paid?)

How many people do you know who have sold their souls so that they can receive a pension in their old age? (And when you've suggested that they ought to have more fun, how many times have you heard them say: 'I'll have plenty of time and money to enjoy myself when I retire.')

Don't let yourself be trapped in the same way.

And if you ARE trapped, don't be afraid to break free.

You only get one chance at living. Don't sell your body, soul and mind so that you can buy an ice cream maker, a time share apartment in Marbella and a three piece suite in mushroom velour. Don't make the mistake of wasting your life on low expectations. Don't let your possessions own you and direct your life.

You may feel that you would like to do something with your life. But you may feel afraid. Dig down into your spirit and you will find dreams that just need dusting off.

Let your dreams out.

Why be afraid? What have you got to lose?

Take life by the scruff of the neck and shake it.

Whatever happens you will not regret the things which go wrong as much as you will regret the things you never do. Failing is no worse than not trying.

The saddest phrase in the English language is 'might have been'. When the game is over your regrets will tell you more about yourself than your accomplishments. Don't make the mistake most people make – of worrying too much and thinking too little.

The secret of life is to be passionate.

If you do not dedicate your life to a cause about which you feel passionate you will eventually ask yourself whether life is worthwhile. And you will not know the answer.

Spend some time deciding what you want to DO with the rest of your life.

And remember that the greatest irony of all is that you need something you are prepared to die for before you can get the most out of life.

With love and thanks for all your lovely letters.

Appendix 2
Author Biography

Sunday Times bestselling author Vernon Coleman qualified as a doctor in 1970 and has worked both in hospitals and as a principal in general practice. Vernon Coleman is a multi-million selling author. He has written over 100 books which have sold over three million copies in the UK, been in bestseller lists around the world and been translated into 26 languages. Several of his books have been on the bestseller lists and in the UK, paperback editions of his books have been published by Pan, Penguin, Corgi, Arrow, Century, RKP, Mandarin and Star among many others. His novel 'Mrs Caldicot's Cabbage War' was turned into a successful, award winning movie, and his play of the same name has been produced by amateur drama societies. He has presented numerous programmes on television and radio, including several series based on his best-selling book Bodypower which was voted one of the 100 most popular books by British readers.

Vernon Coleman has written columns for the Daily Star, Sun, Sunday Express, Planet on Sunday and The People and has contributed over 5,000 articles, columns and reviews to 100 leading British publications including Daily Telegraph, Sunday Telegraph, Guardian, Observer, Sunday Times, Daily Mail, Mail on Sunday, Daily Express, Woman, Woman's Own, Punch and Spectator. His columns and articles have also appeared in hundreds of leading magazines and newspapers throughout the rest of the world. His travel articles were illustrated with his own photographs, and his cartoons have appeared in many magazines. He edited the British Clinical Journal and founded and edited the European Medical Journal. For twenty years he wrote a column which was syndicated to over 40 leading regional newspapers in the UK and to papers all around the world. He was a Professor of Holistic Medical Science and has lectured at three medical schools.

In the UK, Vernon Coleman was the TV AM doctor on breakfast TV and the first networked television Agony Aunt, working on the BBC. Many millions consulted his Telephone Doctor advice lines, and for six years he wrote a monthly newsletter which had subscribers in 17 countries.

Since the early 1990s he has had a website (www.vernoncoleman.com) and the latest figures show that between 25 and 30 million people read his web articles each month. However, for exposing forbidden truths about covid and the toxic covid vaccine, he has been made what George Orwell described as an 'unperson'. For the strange, modern crime of telling the truth he has been banned by YouTube and all social media, libelled by Wikipedia and Google, banned and abused by the mainstream media and, curiously, expelled from the Royal Society of Arts. He was, bizarrely, even banned from watching other people's videos on YouTube.

Vernon Coleman has a medical degree, and an honorary science doctorate. He has worked for the Open University in the UK and was an honorary Professor of Holistic Medical Sciences at the Open International University based in Sri Lanka. He worked as a general practitioner for ten years (resigning from the NHS after being fined for refusing to divulge confidential information about his patients to State bureaucrats) and has organised numerous campaigns both for people and for animals. He has given evidence to both the House of Commons and the House of Lords in the UK. He can ride a bicycle and swim, though not at the same time. He likes animals, cafés and collecting cigarette cards. Vernon Coleman is a bibliophile and has a library larger than most towns. He used to enjoy cricket when it was played as a sport by gentlemen but lost heart when the authorities started painting advertisements on the grass. He loves log fires and making bonfires.

Since 1999 he has been very happily married to the professional artist and author, Donna Antoinette Coleman to whom he is devoted and with whom he has co-written five books. They live in the delightful if isolated village of Bilbury in Devon where they have designed for themselves a unique world to sustain and nourish them in these dark and difficult times. They rarely leave home though when they do it is usually in a 1957 Bentley.

For more information please visit: www.vernoncoleman.com or see his author page on Amazon.

Appendix 3
What the papers say:

(These quotes are included to balance the lies which are now littered throughout the internet.)

'Vernon Coleman writes as a general practitioner who has become disquieted by the all-pervasive influence of the pharmaceutical industry in modern medicine…He describes, with a wealth of illustrations, the phenomena of modern iatrogenesis; but he is also concerned about the wider harm which can result from doctors' and patients' preoccupation with medication instead of with the prevention of disease. He demonstrates, all the more effectively because he writes in a sober, matter-of-fact style, the immense influence exercised by the drug industry on doctors' prescribing habits…He writes as a family doctor who is keenly aware of the social dimensions of medical practice. He ends his book with practical suggestions as to how medical care – in the developing countries as well as in the West – can best be freed from this unhealthy pharmaceutical predominance.' – G.M.Carstairs, The Times Literary Supplement (1975)

'What he says of the present is true: and it is the great merit of the book that he says it from the viewpoint of a practising general practitioner, who sees from the inside what is going on, and is appalled by the consequences to the profession, and to the public.' – Brian Inglis, Punch (1975)

'Dr Coleman writes with more sense than bias. Required reading for any Minister of Health' – Daily Express

'I hope this book becomes a bestseller among doctors, nurses and the wider public…' – Nursing Times

'Dr Coleman's well-coordinated book could not be more timely.' –

Yorkshire Post

'Few would disagree with Dr Coleman that more should be done about prevention.' – The Lancet

'This short but very readable book has a message that is timely. Vernon Coleman's point is that much of the medical research into which money and expertise are poured is useless. At the same time, remedial conditions of mind and body which cause the most distress are largely neglected. This is true.' – Daily Telegraph

'If you believe Dr Vernon Coleman, the main beneficiaries of the hundred million pounds worth of research done in this country each year are certainly not the patients. The research benefits mostly the medical place seekers, who use their academic investigations as rungs on the promotional ladder, or drug companies with an eye for the latest market opening…The future may hold bionic superman but all a nation's physic cannot significantly change the basic mortality statistics except sometimes, to make them worse.' – The Guardian

'Dr Coleman's well-coordinated book could not be more timely.' – Yorkshire Post

'The Medicine Men is well worth reading' – Times Educational Supplement

'Dr Vernon Coleman…is not a mine of information – he is a fountain. It pours out of him, mixed with opinions which have an attractive common sense ring about them.' – Coventry Evening Telegraph

'When the children have finished playing the games on your Sinclair or Commodore Vic 20 computer, you can turn it to more practical purposes. For what is probably Britain's first home doctor programme for computers is now available. Dr Vernon Coleman, one of the country's leading medical authors, has prepared the text for a remarkable series of six cassettes called The Home Doctor Series. Dr Coleman, author of the new book 'Bodypower'…has turned his attention to computers.' – The Times 1983

'The Medicine Men' by Dr Vernon Coleman, was the subject of a 14 minute 'commercial' on the BBC's Nationwide television programme recently. Industry doctors and general practitioners come in for a severe drubbing: two down and several more to go because the targets for Dr Coleman's pen are many, varied and, to say the least, surprising. Take the physicians who carry out clinical trials: many of those, claims the author, have sold themselves to the industry and agreed to do research for rewards of one kind or another, whether that reward be a trip abroad, a piece of equipment, a few dinners, a series of published papers or simply money.' – The Pharmaceutical Journal

'By the year 2020 there will be a holocaust, not caused by a plutonium plume but by greed, medical ambition and political opportunism. This is the latest vision of Vernon Coleman, an articulate and prolific medical author…this disturbing book detects diseases in the whole way we deliver health care.' – Sunday Times (1988)

'…the issues explores he explores are central to the health of the nation.' – Nursing Times

'It is not necessary to accept his conclusion to be able to savour his decidedly trenchant comments on today's medicine…a book to stimulate and to make one argue.' – British Medical Journal

'As a writer of medical bestsellers, Dr Vernon Coleman's aim is to shock us out of our complacency…it's impossible not to be impressed by some of his arguments.' – Western Daily Press

'Controversial and devastating' – Publishing News

'Dr Coleman produces mountains of evidence to justify his outrageous claims.' – Edinburgh Evening News

'Dr Coleman lays about him with an uncompromising verbal scalpel, dipped in vitriol, against all sorts of sacred medical cows.' – Exeter Express and Echo

'Vernon Coleman writes brilliant books.' – The Good Book Guide

'No thinking person can ignore him. This is why he has been for over 20 years one of the world's leading advocates on human and animal rights in relation to health. Long may it continue.' – The Ecologist

'The calmest voice of reason comes from Dr Vernon Coleman.' – The Observer

'A godsend.' – Daily Telegraph

'Dr Vernon Coleman has justifiably acquired a reputation for being controversial, iconoclastic and influential.' – General Practitioner

'Superstar.' – Independent on Sunday

'Brilliant!' – The People

'Compulsive reading.' – The Guardian

'His message is important.' – The Economist

'He's the Lone Ranger, Robin Hood and the Equalizer rolled into one.' – Glasgow Evening Times

'The man is a national treasure.' – What Doctors Don't Tell You

'His advice is optimistic and enthusiastic.' – British Medical Journal

'Revered guru of medicine.' – Nursing Times

'Gentle, kind and caring' – Western Daily Press

'His trademark is that he doesn't mince words. Far funnier than the usual tone of soupy piety you get from his colleagues.' – The Guardian

'Dr Coleman is one of our most enlightened, trenchant and sensitive dispensers of medical advice.' – The Observer

'Vernon Coleman is a leading medical authority and known to millions through his writing, broadcasting and bestselling books.' – Woman's Own

'His book Bodypower is one of the most sensible treatises on personal survival that has ever been published.' – Yorkshire Evening Post

'One of the country's top health experts.' – Woman's Journal

'Dr Coleman is crusading for a more complete awareness of what is good and bad for our bodies. In the course of that he has made many friends and some powerful enemies.' – Western Morning News

'Brilliant.' – The People

'Dr Vernon Coleman is one of our most enlightened, trenchant and sensible dispensers of medical advice.' – The Observer

'The most influential medical writer in Britain. There can be little doubt that Vernon Coleman is the people's doctor.' – Devon Life

'The medical expert you can't ignore.' – Sunday Independent

'A literary genius.' – HSL Newsletter

'I would much rather spend an evening in his company than be trapped for five minutes in a radio commentary box with Mr Geoffrey Boycott.' – Peter Tinniswood, Punch

'Hard hitting...inimitably forthright.' – Hull Daily Mail

'Refreshingly forthright.' – Liverpool Daily Post

'Outspoken and alert.' – Sunday Express

'The man with a mission.' – Morning News

'A good read…very funny and packed with interesting and useful advice.' – The Big Issue

'Dr Coleman gains in stature with successive books' – Coventry Evening Telegraph

'Dr Coleman made me think again.' – BBC World Service

'Marvellously succinct, refreshingly sensible.' – The Spectator

'The living terror of the British medical establishment. A doctor of science as well as a medical graduate. Dr Coleman is probably one of the most brilliant men alive today. His extensive medical knowledge renders him fearless.' – Irish Times

'His future as King of the media docs is assured.' – The Independent

'Britain's leading medical author.' – The Star

'His advice is practical and readable.' – Northern Echo

'The layman's champion.' – Evening Herald

'All commonsense and no nonsense.' – Health Services Management

'One of Britain's leading experts.' – Slimmer Magazine

'The only three things I always read before the programme are Andrew Rawnsley in the Observer, Peter Hitchens in the Mail and Dr Vernon Coleman in The People. Or, if I'm really up against it, just Vernon Coleman.' – Eddie Mair, Presenter on BBC's Radio Four

'Dr Coleman is more illuminating than the proverbial lady with the lamp' – Company Magazine

'Britain's leading health care campaigner.' – The Sun

'What he says is true.' – Punch

'Perhaps the best known health writer for the general public in the world today.' – The Therapist

'The patient's champion. The doctor with the common touch.' – Birmingham Post

'A persuasive writer whose arguments, based on research and experience, are sound.' – Nursing Standard

'Coleman is controversial but respected and has been described in the British press as `the sharpest mind in medial journalism' and `the calmest voice of reason'. – Animals Today

'Vernon Coleman…rebel with a cause.' – Belfast Newsletter

'…presents the arguments against drug based medicine so well, and disturbs a harmful complacency so entertainingly.' – Alternative News

'He is certainly someone whose views are impossible to ignore, with his passionate advocacy of human and animal rights.' – International Journal of Alternative and Complementary Medicine

'The doctor who dares to speak his mind.' – Oxford Mail

'Dr Coleman speaks openly and reassuringly.' – Oxford Times

'He writes lucidly and wittily.' – Good Housekeeping

Note
If you have found this book instructive or amusing please write and post a suitable review. Please don't give me a bad review because

the packaging was damaged or because the book contains nothing about Gloucester Cathedral or fly fishing. Thank you. Your kindness means more to me than I can tell you.